Beyond Basic Dog Training
The Workbook

Diane L. Bauman
Kathy Santo and Dee Zurburg

Alpine
Blue Ribbon Books

An imprint of Alpine Publications, Inc.

**Beyond Basic Dog Training –
THE WORKBOOK**

Copyright 1994 by Diane Bauman, Kathy Santo, and Dee Zurburg

All rights reserved. Except for brief quotations in critical articles or reviews, no part of this book may be reproduced in any manner without prior written permission from the publisher. Write to: Permissions, Alpine Publications, PO Box 7027, Loveland, CO 80537

Cover design: B.J. McKinney

Alpine books are available at special quantity discounts for bulk purchases to clubs, breeders, or for educational use. Special books or book excerpts can also be created to fit special needs.

For details, write or telephone Special Markets, Alpine Publications, PO Box 7027, Loveland, CO 80537; (303) 667-2017

1 2 3 4 5 6 7 8 9 0
Printed in the United States of America.

CONTENTS

ACKNOWLEDGMENTS —   i

FORMS —   ii

INTRODUCTION —   1
    Purpose of this Workbook

THE SUCCESSFUL TRAINER —   2
    What exactly does this mean? * Is this a good question? *
    Walking a straight line * The natural look * Balance your dog

SHOW MODE vs TRAINING MODE —   8
    Increasing and Decreasing speed * Using your eyes

COPING WITH NERVES IN THE RING —   13
    So why be nervous? * Butterflies

GOING OUT TO TRAIN —   15
    The training Plan * Before picking up the leash *
    Now think about time & your dog * On your own *
    Hot tips for Hot climates

HEELING —   22
    The Alphabet * Forward Halt * Do you Panic?

THE FIGURE EIGHT —   33
    Match Game * Learning the figure eight

EXERCISE FINISHED —   36
    Finish

FRONTS —   38

THE STAND —   39

RETRIEVE —   41

DROP ON RECALL – 42
    Getting a dog to drop * Getting a dog to come

THE BROAD JUMP – 46

GLOVES – 47

PIVOT LEFT – 49

SCENT ARTICLES – 50
    Problems * Ask why? * Scenarios * Hidden pictures

GO OUTS – 54
    Teach the dog to leave your side * Teach the dog to go until you tell him to stop * Teach the dog to go in a straight line

UNDERSTANDING PROOFING – 57
    Auditory * Visual * Olfactory * Kinesthetic

MISTAKES DOGS MAKE – 59
    Causing Mistakes * Novice * Open * Utility
    The root of the problem * The weak link

MYSTERY STORIES – 67
    Why doesn't Midnight drop? * Why does he cut the broad jump?
    Why is he not coming? * Clues

THE "W" LEARNING CURVE – 71
    Confusion * Worsens * Improvement * Discourage
    Improves again * Does skill confidently

SOLVING TRAINING PROBLEMS – 77
    Dog behavior * Your behavior * The Gap

PLANNING TO SHOW AT A MATCH SHOW – 82
    Match/Show Log

O. T. CH. – 85
    Requirements * Point Schedule * Summary OTCH Points
    Summary Obedience Record * Summary of Tournaments

WARMING UP A DOG – 91
    The purpose * Evaluate * Show vs Training Mode

KNOWLEDGE OF THE AKC RULES — 95
    Novice * Open * Utility * What is wrong with this picture?

ANCHORING — 99
    Do dogs anchor feelings? * How to anchor a word

HIERARCHY — 101

JUMPING JUMBLE — 102

TO PINCH or NOT TO PINCH — 104
    Shelby & the Poodle * Maggie & a thunder boom
    Sam & the long wet grass * Misha & articles

OBEDIENCE CROSSWORD PUZZLE — 110

PROGRESS CHARTS — 112
    Heeling * Figure 8 * Recall * Down Stays * Sit Stay
    Stand * Finish * Fronts * High & Bar Jumps * Broad Jump
    Retrieve * Retrieve on Flat * Drop on Recall * Directed
    Jumping * Directed Retrieve * Moving Stand * Scent
    Discrimination * Signals * Go–Outs

A DAY AT THE SHOW — 151
    List to improve performance * Things to bring to a dog show

WHERE TO GO FOR TRAINING HELP — 157

THE ANSWERS TO ALL YOUR QUESTIONS — 158
    "Match Show Logs" * Personal Notes

ACKNOWLEDGMENTS

The authors of <u>Beyond Basic Dog Training: The Workbook</u> would like to extend a special word of thanks to:

a) _____ Sherry Palmer –
   for her creative and instructive illustrations.

b) _____ Carol Salzetti –
   for her proof reading expertise.

c) _____ Teresa M. Preciado –
   for months and hours of typesetting, page formatting and design.

d) _____ All the people –
   who took phone messages and hand delivered manuscripts.

CHECK ALL THAT APPLY

ANSWERS: a, b, c and d

THIS Obedience Training Workbook is

FOR: _____

BREED: _____

Age at Start of Training: _____

Temperament: _____

Structural Qualities or Faults:

_____

Handler: _____

Goals for This Dog: _____

Plan to Start Show Career on or About:

_____

It helps to have goals, be focused, and plan ahead.

WHAT IS THE PURPOSE OF THIS WORKBOOK

Have you ever noticed that when you ask a question and get an answer, you more likely to remember and understand that answer than if the information is given to you when you didn't request it? When you listen to a lecture, how much do you really retain? Advertisers realize the impact of questions on the human brain. It is no accident that some of the most successful commercials involved questions like: "Where's the beef?", "Is it soup yet?" and "How do you spell relief?" When we ask a question, we tend to remember the answer.

It has been said that thinking is a process of asking and answering questions. When we think about solving a problem, we ask ourselves many questions: Will this work? What will happen if I try this? What happened the last time when I tried something similar to this?

If we accept that learning involves thinking, and that thinking is asking and answering questions, then it's time we had a book of questions and answers for people who want to learn how to train dogs!

Some people learn by reading and applying what the written word says. Others learn by doing or by visualizing. By using the text: Beyond Basic Dog Training (Howell, Rev. 1992) in conjunction with this workbook, the information on dog training should become readily available to everyone.

In the pages that follow you will find a variety of puzzles, games, and questions designed to get you to learn the art of teaching dog obedience according to the methods outlined in Beyond Basic Dog Training. (Howell, Rev. 1992). In addition, there are charts and tables to help you track your dog's progress through his obedience career. This book is designed so that each dog you are training should have his own workbook. Feel free to write in the workbook since your active participation is essential learning. As you attempt to answer the question, check your responses with the answers in the back of the book. Be prepared to be wrong. Every wrong answer corrected should teach you something. Just like the dogs, we learn by making mistakes. As you correct your mistakes, think about how it feels. Think about how it feels to realize your answer is wrong when you tried so hard to be right! And finally, think about how the dog might feel about making mistakes. Now that you have chosen to train with methods that produce a "thinking dog", it is time to become a thinking handler!

BECOMING A SUCCESSFUL DOG TRAINER

It has been said by experts who study prospering businesses that what makes one person successful and another not, is the ability of the successful person to ask better questions.

What exactly does this mean?

Imagine:

You are training your first dog who happens to be an Irish Terrier. Of course you didn't know that this was not one of the "easily trainable" breeds when you started and you have now struggled through to Utility. Your scores have been high 170's, low 180's, but you are grateful for each and every leg you've earned. Your goal is to put a UD on this Terrier and then start training another dog with whom you can aspire to get high scores. You have been training in Utility in and out of classes for three (3) years. Your dog is now seven (7) years old. A year ago you started showing the dog in Utility and to date you have NQ'd (non-qualified) thirty (30) times. Each time the dog NQ'd (non-qualified) a different exercise. You are discouraged and have even thought about giving up.

BELOW IS A LIST OF QUESTIONS:
Decide which are the good questions which will lead to success!

Is this a ... Good Question?

YES NO

- [ ] [ ] 1. Why did I ever try training an Irish Terrier?
- [ ] [ ] 2. What are the weak links in every exercise my dog makes a mistake on?
- [ ] [ ] 3. Why is this happening to me?
- [ ] [ ] 4. Where can I find an instructor who has trained many different breeds to their UD degrees who could help me?
- [ ] [ ] 5. Why doesn't anything I do ever work out right?
- [ ] [ ] 6. What am I doing differently in practice that makes my dog perform the exercises correctly at home?
- [ ] [ ] 7. Why doesn't anyone in my training club want to help me?
- [ ] [ ] 8. Have I proofed my dog on every exercise, especially the areas that have presented confusion in the ring?
- [ ] [ ] 9. How can I change my training approach to effect a change in my dog's responses?
- [ ] [ ] 10. Where can I find the perfect show where my dog will qualify?

Learn to ask good questions and watch your success rate increase!

(Check the answers at the back of this Workbook, for the correct responses.)

WALKING A STRAIGHT LINE

In order for your dog to heel well with you, and to maintain an ideal 4" distance from your left hip, you must learn to walk in a straight line. You can train your body and thus learn what it <u>feels like</u> to walk straight.

The key to walking straight is your left foot. If your left foot keeps coming down straight in front of itself, then your right foot can't help but come along for the ride. So, as you attempt this next exercise, concentrate <u>only</u> on your left foot.

Exercise For Straight Lines:

1. Locate a parking lot with straight lines painted on it.

2. Visit the parking lot when it is not busy and take along a friend to help you.

3. Position your left foot on a line and look out straight ahead about 8 ft. and tilt your head slightly down. You should now be in the position you would be in, to heel with your dog in a ring.

4. Close your eyes and begin walking.

5. It is your friend's responsibility to yell "STOP" if you get 2 or more feet off the line or if you are walking into something.

6. When your friend says "STOP", freeze, open your eyes and look down at where your feet are in relation to your line. Make a mental note of where you are off, back up, and try again.

It usually takes 6 or 7 times before you have made enough mental adjustments so that you have learned what it feels like to walk a straight line. Once your feet are programmed to walk straight, you can now turn your attention to training the dog.

<u>Observation:</u>

Go to a shopping center.
W A T C H Do you notice how many people walk with their left toe pointed out and to the left. Force yourself to shop through a store with your feet coming down straight (toes pointed in front of you.)

THE <u>NATURAL</u> LOOK

Visual images can help us gain control over how our bodies move. Thoughts stimulate actions. If we think of something scary, our body tenses. If we think of something calming, our muscles relax. While heeling try thinking of the following images, one at a time:

- A. You are walking on a beach in warm, white sand and your steps are so light that you barely make foot prints.

- B. When making a right or left turn, you are riding a bicycle. You lean ever so slightly to keep your balance and there is no point to the turn.

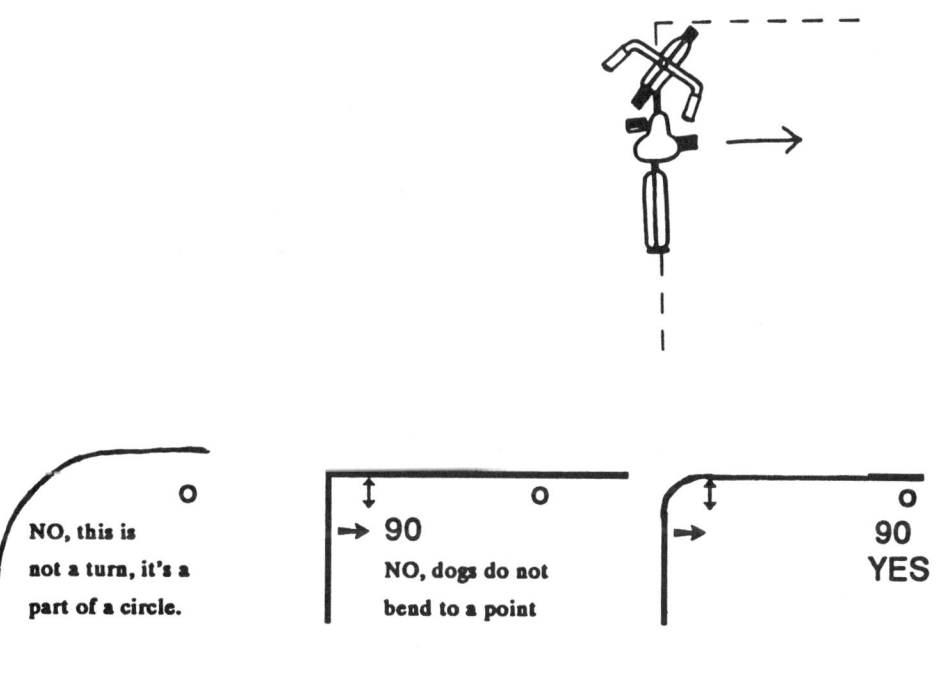

- C. Put a hinge at your waist so that your upper body moves independently from your lower body. (This avoids stiffness.)

Natural Look.... Cont.

D. When going from a normal to a slow, picture yourself coasting down a highway in your car at 65 mph. The speed limit is 55 mph and as you see a police car poking its head out from behind some trees, you immediately take your foot off the accelerator which drops your speed. (No need to put your foot on the brake; decrease smoothly.) To come out of the slow, imagine putting your foot back onto the accelerator gently.

E. Check in with your right hand as you heel. If you find it is clenched or stiff relax it. Relaxing one part of your body helps relax the other parts. Picture a floppy rag doll, then shake out your right hand.

F. Picture the head-bobbing dolls that sit on the back of cars in the window. As you heel, let your head turn (swivel) to look in the direction you are walking. People who have not trained dogs already know how to do this! They usually look where they are going.

BALANCE YOUR DOG....

To help the dog learn the cues for left and right turns and to keep the dog equidistant from your leg, practice doing 5' diameter circles from straight heeling. Just before you go into the circle pull up slowly on a buckle collar to help the dog find his balance. Many beginning dogs fall on their handlers (resulting in a bump) as they lose their balance on a turn. Pulling straight up over the dog's head in a slower, steady pull (not a jerk) helps the dog find his balance on the turn.

Imagine yourself riding a two-wheel bicycle. Now think about the balance you would need if you were to turn that bicycle in a 5' diameter circle.

People who ride horses understand the importance of balancing a horse around a circle and in turns. An unbalanced horse is more likely to fall in a turn. Dogs also falling in turns. They fall into you (bump) and away from you (wide).

SHOW MODE vs TRAINING MODE

When we heel a dog in the ring, we do not stare at the dog to make direct eye contact. This would be judged as guiding your dog. Very few dogs can look into your eyes and maintain heel position when your head is facing forward. For most dogs, it is impossible to make eye contact and keep their "head and shoulders" in line with your left hip at the same time. When we look ahead about 8' and slightly lower our eyes we can see a vague outline of the dog's head with our peripheral vision. This we call "Show Mode".

When we heel with a dog in training, we turn our heads sharply to the left so that we can clearly see every hair on the dog's head. It is now increasingly important that our left foot is trained to walk in a straight line. When we look intensely at a dog while heeling, we call it "Training Mode".

Using the words 'show' or 'training': Fill in the blanks below:

When we first start training a dog, we are always in 1._____ mode. As the dog is capable of giving us 100 % attention at all three speeds, we will from time to time, take a few steps in 2._____ mode. When we first start showing the dog at match shows, we will want to use 3. _____ mode. As we get closer to the day of showing at a licensed trial we will want to practice match showing in 4._____ mode. Whenever we warm up a dog we begin with 5._____ mode and then switch to 6._____ mode. It is not necessary to halt when switching from training mode to 7._____ mode and back again. A dog well trained should not change his heeling as the trainer switches from training mode to 8._____ mode.

(Check the answer at the back of this Workbook, for the correct responses.)

INCREASING AND DECREASING SPEED

Most people are fairly adept at walking until they learn to train dogs. Getting in the habit of looking at your dog to train him distorts a person's natural balance. All too often, as you start to get ready to show and learn SHOW MODE, you no longer know how to walk naturally. You become stiff and upright, which makes transitions difficult.

Let's analyze walking:

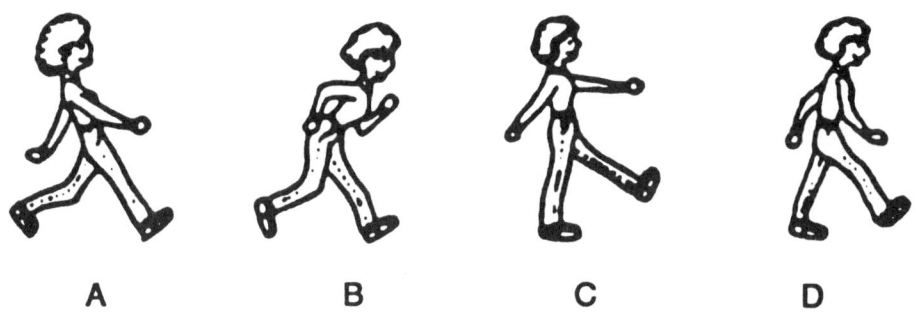

   A   B   C   D

[1] — Which of the above looks most natural if you were walking? If you guessed D, you are correct. When we walk, our weight is slightly in front of our vertical line. Think of the vertical line as a pole running through your body from top to bottom.. almost like a pole through a carousel horse.

As you begin to heel, your weight should be slightly forward of this vertical line.

[2] — As the judge says forward, what is likely to happen if you are standing totally vertical?

      A. Your dog will not pay attention.
      B. You will be off balance to start and your dog will probably start into a forge without you.
      C. The judge will consider it "training in the ring."
      D. All of the above.

It is easy to continue moving at a steady pace as long as your weight remains in front of the vertical.

Increasing & Decreasing...(cont.)

Now think about this:

[3] – Why do people get "stuck" on about turns?

    A. They hesitate to wait for the dog to catch up.
    B. They forget their footwork.
    C. They stand up straight which makes it more difficult to move forward, because their weight is not in front of the verticals.
    D. They are wearing shoes with gripping soles.
    E. They don't turn their head to look where they are going.

Anytime you want to increase speed with your dog you should have your weight in front of the vertical. Anytime you want to decrease speed ... you want to bring your weight back to vertical, or slightly behind it for the slow.

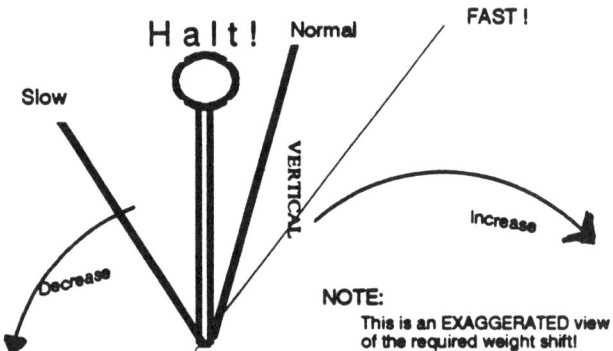

Using the letter "I" for increase of speed and the letter "D" for decrease of speed decide which applies to the following:

[4] – The judge calls: "I" or "D"

    Normal.....Halt!   _____
    Normal...Fast!   _____
    Fast....Normal!   _____
    Normal.......Slow!   _____
    Slow......Normal!   _____
    Halt! Forward...   _____

(Check the answers at the back of this Workbook, for the correct responses.)

USING YOUR EYES

Your eyes play an important role in dog training. They can be used to guide the dog or to direct the dog. A dog who has been taught to pay attention notices where you are looking. For example: By looking at where a dumbbell lands, you can help a dog search in the right spot. By focusing your eyes on the high jump you can help direct a dog back over the high jump.

Eyes can be used in different ways. If you intently focus on a light switch on the wall so that you see little else in the room, it is called   HARD EYES. If you look at the light switch but relax and let yourself see peripherally around the room as well, you would be using   SOFT EYES   Both HARD EYES and soft eyes can be useful at different times in training.

Think about the following situations and decide what kind of eyes would be most helpful:

    (circle one)

1. Teaching a dog to pay attention while moving when you are in training mode.

    SOFT EYES   HARD EYES

2. As a dog comes into you on a front.
   (note: you are not dropping your head as the dog comes in.)

    SOFT EYES   HARD EYES

3. Heeling in a ring situation in show mode.

    SOFT EYES   HARD EYES

4. Teaching a dog the utility hand signals.

    SOFT EYES   HARD EYES

5. Doing the utility hand signals in a ring where you must see the judge give you a signal before you signal the dog.

    SOFT EYES   HARD EYES

6. Giving a dog a signal to a glove.

    SOFT EYES   HARD EYES

EYES.... (cont.)

7. Sending a dog to the article pile.

    SOFT EYES   HARD EYES

8. Sending a dog on Go Out.

    SOFT EYES   HARD EYES

9. Giving a signal direction on directed jumping.

    SOFT EYES   HARD EYES

10. Sending the dog on a retrieve on flat.

    SOFT EYES   HARD EYES

11. Sending the dog on a retrieve over high jump.

    SOFT EYES   HARD EYES

12. Sending the dog on the broad jump.

    SOFT EYES   HARD EYES

13. Calling a dog on the recall.

    SOFT EYES   HARD EYES

14. Standing opposite the dog on Novice Sits and Downs.

    SOFT EYES   HARD EYES

15. Facing the dog after leaving on the moving stand for exam.

    SOFT EYES   HARD EYES

(Check the answers at the back of this Workbook, for the correct responses.)

COPING WITH NERVES IN THE RING

I. Showing dogs is a relatively safe sport.
Which of the following is true?

_____ 1. You cannot fall off of a dog like you can if you ride horses.

_____ 2. Handler's who show dogs who NQ (non-qualify) exercises in the ring are penalized and fined by the AKC.

_____ 3. Most people who show dogs, have perfect dogs and expect to score a 200 frequently.

_____ 4. Even the top obedience dogs make simple mistakes in the ring.

_____ 5. It is unlikely that you will ever be physically injured by a judge in an obedience ring.

_____ 6. Other exhibitors hate people whose dogs fail classes.

_____ 7. It is possible not to place 1 – 4 in a class and still win an award.

_____ 8. If your dog fails a class or works poorly, there is always another show you can go to.

_____ 9. Anything below a score of 197 is failing.

_____ 10. Dogs who score low will always score low.

So why be nervous?

(Check the answers at the back of this Workbook, for the correct responses.)

Nerves...cont.

BUTTERFLIES !!

When you feel the "butterflies" in your stomach, instead of saying to yourself, "Oh, I'm so nervous," try saying, "Oh, I'm so excited to be showing!" Most people get a thrill or a rush of adrenaline before they walk in the ring. If we didn't get some exciting feeling we would probably take up a different hobby. If you get so "excited" that your body trembles and you feel nauseous it is probably because you are forgetting to breathe. Your body is trying to tell you that oxygen is still required. Try taking slow, deep breaths, as you stand up and put a smile on your face. It's difficult to be too terrorized when you are smiling. Then, start walking. Practice your footwork or heel with your dog if he needs to be worn down or warmed up. Focus your thoughts on rhythm, what the pattern is and review your visual images that help keep heeling smooth.

You will probably find that once you enter the ring and begin the heeling pattern your panic leaves. The only time you feel over anxious in the ring is when you stop walking or working with the dog and your mind wanders. Below is a list of thoughts that might enter into your head while in the ring. Put a line through the ones you <u>shouldn't</u> be thinking.

1. One, Two, One, Two, ...(Rhythm)
2. "T.V.", Footwork, come out on the same line.
3. That's a crooked sit.
4. He's lagging.
5. The judge's pencil just moved.
6. Keep feet together.
7. Glide into the slow.
8. Weight in front of the vertical.
9. He was wide on that about turn.
10. Take my time.

Your brain is like a computer. You can control what you think. Tell your brain positive, helpful things that it should think and it wouldn't think about things that will upset you!

Make a list of other good thoughts you should have in the ring !

1. _____
2. _____
3. _____
4. _____

(Check the answers at the back of this Workbook, for the correct responses.)

GOING OUT TO TRAIN

BEFORE YOU PICK UP THE LEASH......
THE TRAINING PLAN

Answer the following: (LIST ONLY ONE)

1) What exercises are we having trouble learning? (We are caught in a learning stage)

    1. _____

2) What exercise (if any) is it time to start teaching?

    2. _____

3) What exercise does the dog understand, but needs polish?

    3. _____

4) What exercise does the dog particularly enjoy doing?

    4. _____

Since we usually work on heeling as well as the other exercises, decide what area of heeling you want to focus on (figure eight is viewed as an exercise, not heeling.)   Pick one to three of the following:

A. Attention at the sit

B. Attention while moving

C. TIming of halts

D. Halts immediately following turns

E. Change of Pace

  (Downward transition, i.e. Fast to normal, normal to slow, slow to halt.) *

F. Change of Pace

  (Upward transition, i.e. start to normal, normal to fast, slow to normal, slow to fast.)

G. About Turns — understanding footwork.

H. About Turns — for rhythm

I. About Turns — for equidistant of dog from handler

  (You may have to hold the dog off your leg.)

J. About Turns — up against the wall.

  * Executing a halt from a slow, helps the dog and
  you to understand the timing and cue for the halt.

GOING OUT....Cont'

K. Right Turns —

(Make sure you work them away from barriers to test to see if the dog really understands the cue. Try doing a 100 ft. straight line of heeling at a normal in rhythm. Then do a right turn with no barrier. Did the dog catch the cue? If not, repeat the exercise and help the dog with your voice.)

L. Left Turns —

Working on getting the dog to notice the cue and stay equidistant from your left leg. If you are getting a bump check out the following:

                                           (OK?)

1. Your footwork. _____
2. Dog's head up _____
   (attention and balance)
3. Is dog in heel position _____
   going into the turn?

BUMPS ON LEFT TURNS USUALLY INDICATE A FORGING DOG!

Transitions —

Practice certain difficult transitions in heeling. Certain maneuvers are easy until you are asked to do them following other maneuvers:

    a.   fast, normal, halt (into a barrier at times)
    b.   fast, normal, about turn
    c.   fast, normal, about turn, halt
    d.   fast, normal, left turn
    e.   forward, halt
    f.   forward, slow
    g.   forward, fast
    h.   slow, normal, right turn
    i.   left turn, fast
    j.   about turn, halt

5) Areas of heeling I want to work on.   5. _____
                                                                       _____

BEFORE YOU PICK UP THE LEASH...... (cont.)

Look at the exercises and parts of heeling you have decided to work on. These will be what you have written in on lines 1 – 5. Now put them in the order you want to work in.

Consider the following:

- Should the dog do heeling first to wake up and establish rhythm and attention between us?
- Is there another exercise that I am more likely to get the dog to make a mistake in if I do it first?
- Do I want to encourage a mistake at this time or, do I prefer to keep it easy and build confidence?
- Is there an exercise that is likely to stress the dog so I should do it near the end of the lesson?
- What exercise will the dog enjoy most that I should do last to leave a positive memory in the dog's mind?

Research tells us that what people learn first and last in a lesson is what they remember best.

Assuming the same is true for dogs, how would you best order today's lesson?

TRAINING PLAN

ORDER OF LESSON:
1. _____
2. _____
3. _____
4. _____
5. _____

NOW THINK ABOUT TIME
and Your Dog.

1) How long do you have to work your dog today? 1. _____

2) Is the dog up and energetic, or is he tired and lacking drive? 2. _____

3) Would the dog benefit from a short run before you work to either calm him down or wake him up? 3. _____

4) Would it be to your advantage to work the dog as soon as you exercise him so he can put whatever energy he has into his work? 4. _____

While we write a TRAINING PLAN, we don't always get a chance to work on everything we had planned. If you hit a problem you didn't expect or if the dog takes longer to figure something out, you may not have time to complete what you had planned.

FOLLOWING TRAINING TAKE A MOMENT to –

1. Write down what you did.
2. Make notes about the dog's reactions and progress.

FOLLOWING TRAINING

Exercises Completed: **NOTES:**

While your training session is still fresh in your mind you might want to write the Training Plan for your next session. Refer to the beginning of this chapter.

O N Y O U R O W N !

Many people, due to a variety of reasons, must train without an instructor or training club. First of all, don't despair! There are more people who train alone than you may think. Here are a few helpful hints:

1. To check fronts and finishes a full length mirror, long windows in stores, or even sliding glass doors will provide a "looking glass".

2. You need to see what you look like during heeling, signals etc., etc. Rent or buy a video camera and have a friend (or use a tripod) tape you. Then watch the tape and make notes on what is good and what needs improvement.

3. To have a different scent on your articles, take them with you on errands. Ask a store clerk, or a person on the street to scent them. You may get some strange looks, but you'll also get new scents!

4. For distractions, go to public places, parks that allow dogs, busy neighborhoods with children. For large, lined areas to help with straight heeling, choose parking lots (churches, grocery stores, malls) during slow times (evenings). Children often like to help you train dogs. They can be taught to proof.

5. If possible, plan on traveling once a month to a training club. Even though the ride may be a long one, your dog and you will benefit from the indoor practice, distractions and group exercises.

6. Find a training buddy. There may be someone near you who is training their dog for titles just like you! If there isn't, encourage a friend with a dog to go with you on a few training sessions. Who knows, they may get hooked, too!

ON YOUR OWN ..... cont.

** HOT TIPS FOR PEOPLE IN VERY HOT CLIMATES **

1. Find a training building. If there is no organized club, get a few friends together and try to rent an empty air conditioned building. Charge for memberships and run through time and you will probably make some money.

2. For outside training, train early in the a.m. or late in the evening.

3. If training on a parking lot, check the temperature of the pavement first.

4. Find shady areas, such as a cluster of trees, covered parking garages or even your own garage.

5. Make sure to carry plenty of cold water. Wet towels or towel coats soaked in ice water can help keep a dog's temperature down. Remember that dogs don't sweat through their skin. By wetting them down, the evaporating water will cool the body.

6. Work in short sessions, then cool the dog down.

7. Be careful to park in the shade, use space blankets (to reflect the sun off the cars) and pay attention to the dogs you may be leaving in the car as you work another one.

HEELING

Answer all that apply!

1. How would you *best* describe heel position? _____

   a. A dog moving parallel to a handler's left hip, neither forging nor lagging.

   b. A dog looking up whose paws are always even with the handler's left hip.

   c. A dog whose head and shoulder (usually this is his ear) is even with the handler's left hip and remains equidistant from the handler no more than 4 inches away, nor close enough to cause interference.

   d. An attentive dog whose head and shoulders are even with the handlers left leg.

   e. All of the Above.

2. In order for a dog to sit straight in heel position, which of the following must occur? _____

   a. The dog must be paying attention by looking into the handler's eyes

   b. The dog must be in heel position (parallel to the handler) at the time of the HALT.

   c. The dog must know from the cue that the handler is stopping.

   d. The dog must be paying attention to some part of the handler's left side.

   e. The handler must stop by slowly coming to a HALT.

Answer
TRUE or FALSE

3. Heel position is slightly different for small dogs. _____

4. All Border Collies heel forged because of their structure. _____

HEELING..... (cont.)

5. If a dog has a lot of coat, and the coat touches the handler's left leg, this is not considered crowding. _____

6. Dogs must change gait when going from normal to fast. _____

7. Drifting left into a dog helps correct crowding. _____

8. Halting on your right foot is an AKC rule. _____

9. The fast and slow can be done the entire length of a ring if a judge chooses to do so. _____

10. Dogs who pace instead of trot have a more difficult time heeling because their weight is all on one side; this makes turning more difficult. _____

11. Once your dog is trained to heel and has a C.D. you should no longer practice on-leash heeling. _____

12. You should never practice off-leash heeling. _____

13. At a normal pace it is ideal for your dog to be trotting and for you to be moving at a brisk pace. _____

14. Heeling a dog on a loose leash helps define heel position.

15. Handler increasing speed (i.e. lengthening steps) on left turns makes it easier for the dog to stay in heel position.

(Check the answers at the back of this Workbook, for the correct responses.)

HEELING THE ALPHABET

Heeling patterns can be described in terms of the shape of a letter.

For example, many Novice patterns follow the shape of a capital "L".

Fig. 1

A Novice "L" Pattern   (x=halt)

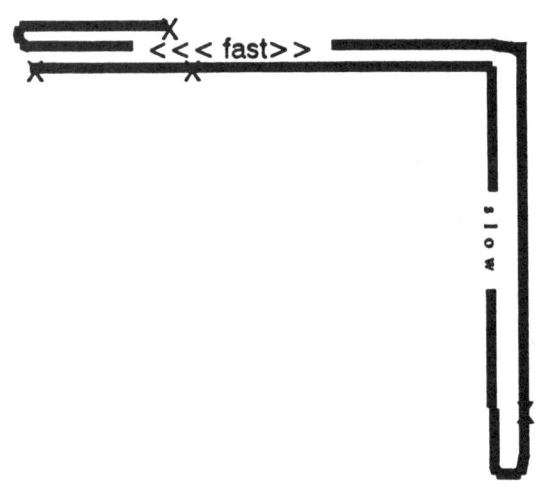

In Open, you frequently find an "F" pattern, or in this case, an inverted "F".

Fig. 2

An Open "F" Pattern

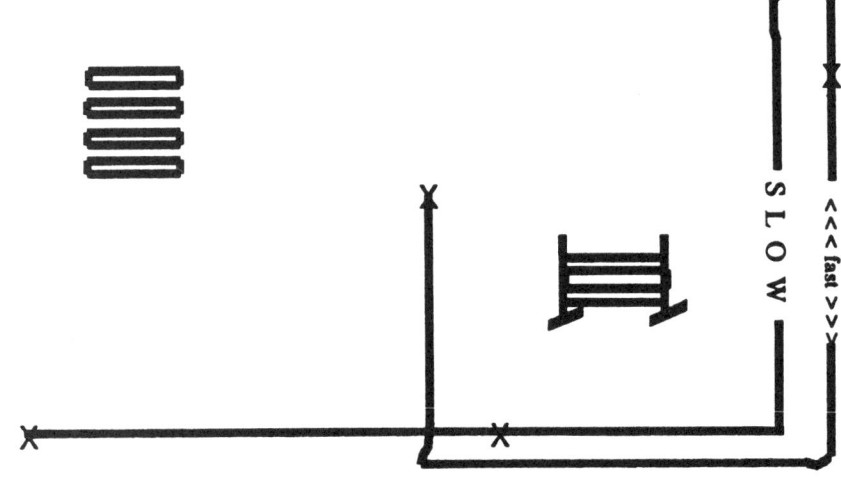

Alphabet...... cont.

In Utility, because of the positions of the jumps, a "T" shape is common.

Fig. 3
A Utility "T" Pattern

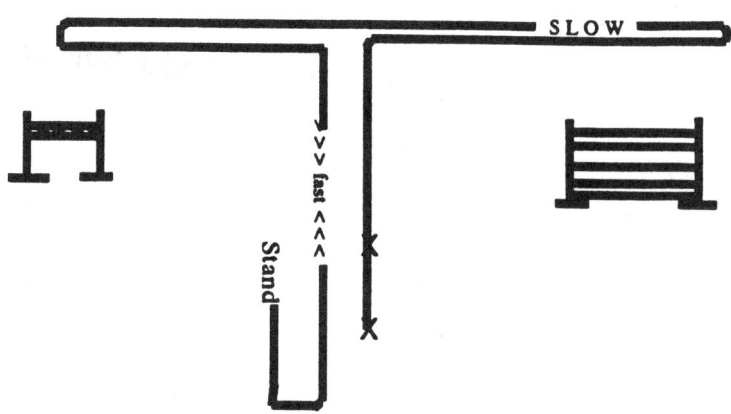

Thinking of heeling in terms of letters of the alphabet helps a handler walk a straight line. When working without a ring set-up, heeling patterns of letter helps you orient yourself on an open field or parking lot.

To avoid practicing the same patterns over and over again, try heeling letters of the alphabet that are <u>not</u> commonly found in the ring:

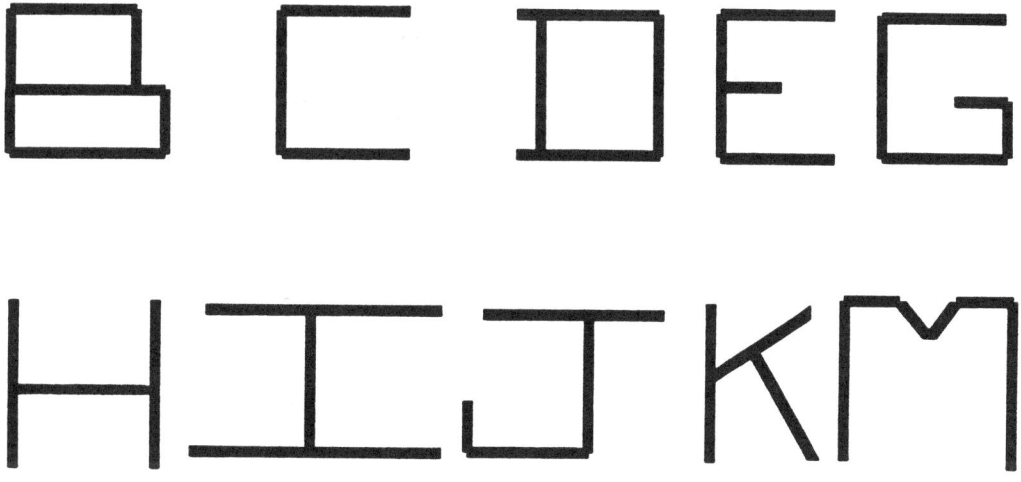

Alphabet...... cont.

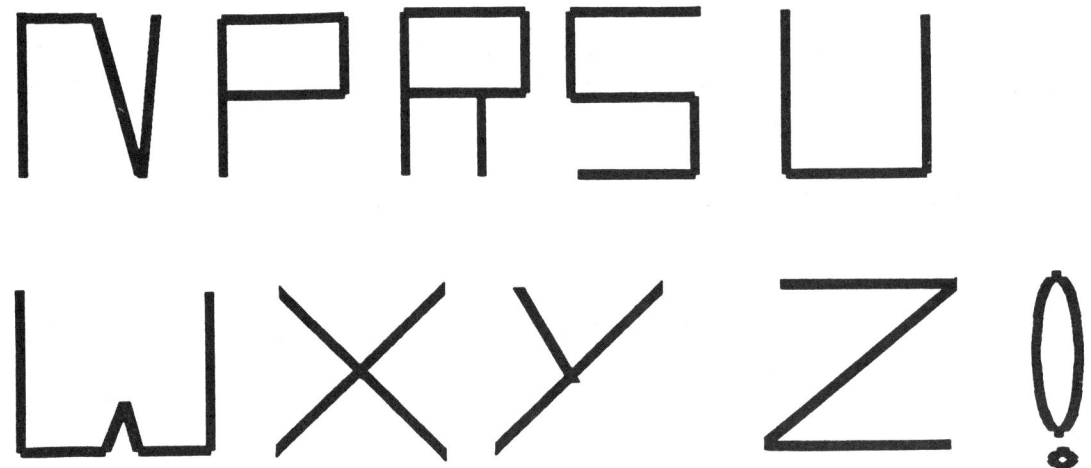

Exercise:
Map out a pattern below with three (3) halts. a fast, a slow and turns, base on one of the block letters above. Refer to figures 1, 2 & 3 as models.

"FORWARD, HALT!"

The most common sequence of commands at the beginning of any heeling pattern is, "Forward ➡➡➡➡➡■Halt!" More dogs sit crooked on this first halt than on any other sit in the heeling pattern.

1. What makes the first halt after only 5 – 12 heeling steps so difficult?

    a. ☐ It tests the dog's reflexes and knowledge of start and stop cues.

    b. ☐ The dog and handler have not had enough steps to establish a rhythm yet.

    c. ☐ The handler is particularly tense because it is the beginning of the class.

    d. ☐ The handler never gets to a normal speed because he/she is anticipating having to halt quickly.

    e. ☐ All of the above.

2. What can the handler do to get a more accurate "Forward, Halt"?

    a. At the start of the heeling pattern the handler can mentally pretend that the staring sit in the ring is <u>not</u> the start of the pattern, but is in fact, one of many halts in a longer heeling pattern. This will help the handler get a rhythm early on in the pattern.

    b. The handler can practice a forward,
    One step halt
    two step halt
    three step halt
    four step halt
    five step halt
    six step halt
    seven step halt
    ⬧
    ⬧
    ⬧
    ⬧
    twelve step halt
    So that no matter how many steps are given, the handler knows the dog has practiced the sequence.

    c. The handler can count the halt, one, two rhythm of heeling.

    d. All of the above.

(Check the answers at the back of this Workbook, for the correct responses.)

DO YOU PANIC!!
When you hear the judge say 'H A L T !'?

If so, you are not alone. Most people are nervous in a situation where they feel they are being judged. Big men and women dressed with authority, holding the dangerous clipboard are very intimidating to poor little exhibitors. How can the exhibitor learn to function effectively in a judgmental situation?

   First, shrink the judge:

Close your eyes and picture an empty ring. Now put the SCARY JUDGE in the center of the ring. Keeping your eyes closed have someone slowly read you the following instructions:

1. If your picture is in color, make it black and white.

2. Push the judge into the corner of the ring far away from where you are.

Panic...Cont'

3. Shrink the judge down in SIZE until he or she is about 3 feet tall.

4. Dress the judge in blue jeans and a silly doggie T–Shirt.

5. Turn the lights down in the ring until you can barely see the judge.

Now Open Your Eyes.

Repeat steps 1–5 with your eyes open.
Now have someone call commands for you.
The judge should feel less threatening.

Panic...Cont'

Second, learn the code to 'HALT!':

There are four different places on straight heeling that a judge can call a halt. They are:

1. Before you step down on your right foot.

2. After you have stepped down on your right foot.

3. Before you have stepped down on your left foot.

4. After you have stepped down on your left foot.

Depending on how fast you are going and when the judge calls a halt will determine how many steps occur before you actually stop moving. This is usually between 2 and 4 steps. There is nothing in the AKC rule book which dictates how many steps are permitted before a halt. However, an excessive number of <u>slower</u> steps will be penalized as the judge will consider it an "aid to the dog" instead of a natural, smooth, halt. Too abrupt a stop can also cost points if the judge considers it to be "unnatural".

To accomplish a smooth, natural halt, when the judge says, "HALT", picture one of the following:

1. A plane coming in for a perfect, smooth landing.

2. A bird gracefully landing on a lake.

P A N I C ... (Cont.)

3. A car smoothly coming to a halt at a stop light.

Practice having someone yell "HALT: with authority and seeing your picture of one of the above.

THE HALT CODE:

Ideally the handler wants to stop on his right foot and bring his left foot up to meet the right. (in other words, close with the left.)

To accomplish this, when the judge commands, "HALT!" you repeat halt to yourself as soon as you step down on your left foot. Then say ONE as you step down on to you right foot and then TWO as you close with your left foot. Try it slowly at first and see how easy it is to make the halt.

The sequence of saying, "HALT, ONE, TWO." will give you the rhythm needed to accomplish a smooth halt with proper cues for the dog.

Practice this "HALT, ONE, TWO" without the dog first. Then see if you can find the rhythm with the dog.

Remember: Your weight (upper body) comes back to a vertical position on the halt. (see pg. 9.)

Under normal circumstances every command you hear a judge say in the ring should first be acknowledged by you mentally and then executed. For example, if a judge commands, "FORWARD", you should first say forward to yourself and then command the dog to heel. It takes your brain less than one second to acknowledge the command. By acknowledging a command first, you will avoid stepping before you are ready or reacting with the wrong cue for your dog.

P A N I C ... (Cont.)

Fill in the blanks below:

1. The Judge says "FORWARD".   You say to yourself:_____
2. The Judge says "HALT".   You say to yourself:_____
3. The Judge says "RIGHT TURN".   You say to yourself:_____
4. The judge says "FAST".   You say to yourself:_____
5. The Judge says "ABOUT TURN".   You say to yourself:_____
6. The Judge says "SEND YOUR DOG". You say to yourself:_____
7. The Judge says "THROW IT".   You say to yourself:_____
8. The Judge says "LEAVE YOUR DOG". You say to yourself:_____

(Check the answers at the back of this Workbook, for the correct responses.)

THE FIGURE EIGHT

How your dog would describe the exercise:

"My handler told me to 'SIT' and I did, making sure to look up and pay attention so I would hear the next command. I noticed two 'strange people' standing close to us as I heard the next command, 'HEEL'. I knew this meant we were moving forward in a straight line. No sooner did I stand up and start to heel then my handler cued me to turn left. I leaned away from my handler's hip which necessitated me lifting my head up a little higher so as not to collide. The cues came repeatedly: 'Left Turn, Left Turn,' until we had made a small half circle. With every cue step I pulled my head up and off of my handler, and stepped sideways with my rear which enabled me to stay parallel with my handler's body. I was careful to slow down my stride a little which made it possible for me to stay in heel position and not forge. Finally, we straightened out, but only for a few steps. The next thing I knew, I was being cued to the right. I quickly increased my speed, leaned into my front right leg and pushed with my rear as my hind legs crossed over to enable me to stay parallel with my handler. We made a similar semicircle to the right and again straightened out for a few steps. Finally there was the cue to 'Halt' and I sighed with relief. This is not an easy exercise to master. Things happen very quickly and there is so much I have to do."

I. CONNECT THE DOTS TO DRAW A CORRECT FIGURE EIGHT:

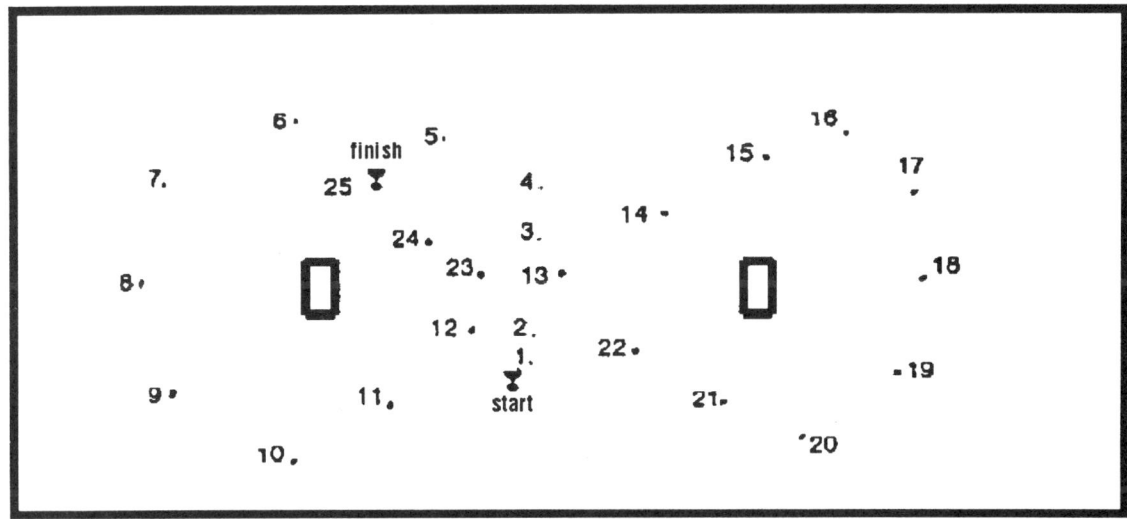

THE FIGURE EIGHT
MATCH GAME

II.

DIRECTIONS:
Read all the phrases on the left and on the right of the center line. Then choose which phrase on the right best completes the beginning sentence on the left.

1. Single Track

2. Start off on your right foot

3. The dog should be paying attention, looking up and pulling his head away from the handler

4. Step off on your left foot in a straight line

5. The dog's feet crossing in the rear

6. The dog must push with his rear and lean in on his front right leg towards the handler

A. when starting the figure eight.

B. the entire figure 8.

C. if stopped on a curve.

D. when the dog is on the inside of the figure 8.

E. when the dog is on the outside of the figure 8.

F. keeps the dog in heel position.

(Check the answers at the back of this Workbook, for the correct responses.)

FIGURE EIGHT...(cont.)

III. LEARNING THE FIGURE EIGHT AND THEN TEACHING IT TO THE DOG!

Ideally the handler learns how to walk the figure eight first and then teaches the maneuvers to the dog. Below are a list of steps in the process of learning the figure eight and teaching it to the dog.

See if you can put them in the order you would want to complete each step:

ORDER	STEP
1. ___	A. The handler teaches the dog to increase speed on the outside curve and decrease speed on the inside curve. By going slowly when the dog is on the inside, and by taking short, running steps when the dog is on the outside of the eight and verbally encouraging the dog to speed up, the dog learns to change pace. All of this is done on a taut lead so the dog cannot get out of heel position. DATE COMPLETED: ___
2. ___	B. The handler assumes a steady speed and verbally cues the dog to slow down or speed up around the curves. The handler points to heel position as the dog heels around the eight. DATE COMPLETED: ___
3. ___	C. The handler learns to single track the figure eight with the appropriate shift of weight. This is learned by "flying around the posts" (see page 91 of – <u>Beyond Basic Dog Training.</u>) DATE COMPLETED: ___
4. ___	D. The handler works the figure eight with the dog tied to him. This simulates off-leash heeling. All help and corrections are made with the handler's left hand. DATE COMPLETED: ___
5. ___	E. The handler uses a dowel to help the dog learn to move his rear and bend into a correct parallel heel position. DATE COMPLETED: ___

(Check the answers at the back of this Workbook, for the correct responses.)

Exercise FINISHed

A finish from the dog's point of view:

I had just sat "Front", my eyes looking at the spot that my owner points to in practice. I awaited her command to "Heel". The judge said, "Finish", and I resisted the urge to do so without her command, as I knew what was expected of me. She said my name and "Heel" and I got up and briskly trotted around her, being sure to keep my eyes up and looking for heel position. As I was behind her, I heard some interesting sound from the ring next to us, but I continued my journey around until I came into heel position. I was careful to bring my entire body all the way around her, because if I didn't, I might wind up in a crooked sit. After I completed my finish, and continued to look at heel position, the judge said "Exercise Finished".

TRUE OR FALSE AND WHY

1. A dowel can be used to tap the chest of a dog that forges on the sit portion of the finish.

   _____

2. The key to the finish exercise is to teach the dog to go way behind you so that he will come up into a straight sit.

   _____

3. Teaching the finish in which the dog goes around behind you into heel position gives you a better chance of a straight sit.

   _____

4. Small dogs may require two steps backwards and two steps forward to get them up and moving on a finish.

   _____

5. The finish hand signal for Utility is taught at the same time as the finish exercise because the leash is held in your right hand.

   _____

6. Dogs generally learn the finish exercise in one or two sessions.

   _____

(Check the answers at the back of this Workbook, for the correct responses.)

F I N I S H !

We use the "around" finish because it gives a better chance of a straight sit.

The following answers pertain to the "around" finish.

Draw a line to connect the correct answers:

1) To encourage a dog to come around looking up, you can..

2) In training as the dog comes around on the finish, the handler should..

3) For some large dogs, instead of taking one step backwards and one forward, you may..

4) As the dog is coming around into heel position you should never..

5) The "key" to getting a straight sit on the finish is..

6) To finish your dog and then take off walking encourages a dog to..

7) The rules state that a dog should come _____ around on the finish.

A. Teaching a dog to finish with his head up.

B. Point out heel position with the left hand.

C. Take two steps back and two forward.

D. Snap him up into heel.

E. Hold a motivator, such as toys or food.

F. Hold the dog's head up.

G. Smartly

H. Come around briskly.

A straight finish requires many weeks until it is perfected.

Be Patient!!

(Check the answers at the back of this Workbook, for the correct responses.)

Teaching Fronts

TRUE or FALSE

___1) Teaching a dog to sit straight in front of you is a gradual process that takes months to perfect.

___2) As the dog comes in to you, stepping back will help straighten the sit front.

___3) Guides are used to help a dog think about front about 4 feet before he must sit.

___4) Dogs with long backs are easier to teach to sit straight in front.

___5) A dog must first learn to look with his eyes at some point on the midline of your body before he can learn to fold his rear straight under him.

___6) A dog who rocks back on a sit is not a problem on the sit front.

___7) The handler makes use of his knees and feet to help the dog learn to line up his rear with his front.

___8) It doesn't matter where the dog is looking as he comes into you, only that he must look up at your face when he sits.

___9) Dogs should be taught to sit in the space between your legs.

___10) Bending your knees helps keep a dog from sitting too close.

___11) The command used when teaching fronts should be the same command used on a recall.

___12) A dog must understand that he must sit, following a recall before he can learn to sit straight.

___13) Pulling a dog by the collar into a straight sit front will teach him where he needs to sit.

___14) Working fronts in a too serious or corrective way will cause a dog to slow down the last few steps on a recall.

(Check the answers at the back of this Workbook, for the correct responses.)

Clarify THE STAND

Obedience now has three exercises where the dog must stand (one in Novice, two in Utility.)

These exercises are:

(N) 1) **N**ovice Stand for Examination.
(S) 2) Stand in **S**ignal exercise (Utility.)
(M) 3) **M**oving Stand for Exam (Utility.)

It is important that you as the handler and trainer clearly understand how these exercises are similar and how they are different.

Using the letters:

(N) for **N**ovice Stand
(S) for **S**ignal Stand
(M) for **M**oving Stand

See if you can determine which exercise is being described below. (Circle all that apply)

1. We stand the dog using hand signal and voice commands.

    N   S   M

2. We stand the dog by giving a signal with our right hand while at the same time, stepping forward on our right foot.

    N   S   M

3. We stand the dog as he is heeling.

    N   S   M

4. Once the dog is standing, he is examined by the judge.

    N   S   M

Clarify the stand.... Cont.

5. The exam from the judge includes touching the dog's legs.

    N   S   M

6. After we stand the dog we stop moving and bring our left foot up to meet our right.

    N   S   M

7. We may reposition the dogs feet after he stands up if he is not standing squarely.

    N   S   M

8. After we stand the dog we continue moving and the dog stops in a standing position.

    N   S   M

9. Following the stand the dog is called to front.

    N   S   M

10. Following the stand, we return to heel position.

    N   S   M

11. Following the stand, the dog comes directly to heel position.

    N   S   M

12. We stand the dog using only the hand signal.

    N   S   M

(Check the answers at the back of this Workbook, for the correct responses.)

RETRIEVE !!

{ Confucius say – "dumbbell in mouth gets hand off ear!"}

Each retrieve step is crucial to the eventual success and reliability of the retrieve.
DO   NOT   skip steps, and when in doubt, – help instead of correct.

Put the following retrieve steps in the order you would teach them. (1–9)

a. _____ The dog will voluntarily open his mouth upon feeling the pressure of the dumbbell on his teeth.

b. _____ The dog, after reaching for dumbbell, will hold it in mouth for 1 minute without chewing or mouthing.

c. _____ The dog will retrieve a leash–length off the ground and return and sit.

d. _____ The dog will reach one inch for the dumbbell.

e. _____ The dog will retrieve the dumbbell from the floor with the handler's hand on it.

f. _____ The dog will allow the handler to open his mouth, upon feeling the pressure of the dumbbell against his lip.

g. _____ The dog will reach six inches at, above and below his eye level.

h. _____ The dog will hold the dumbbell while standing and moving.

i. _____ The dog will retrieve at leash length when the dumbbell is next to a distraction.

(Check the back of this Workbook, for the correct responses.)

DROP ON RECALL

As you teach the drop on recall you will encounter two major learning stages:

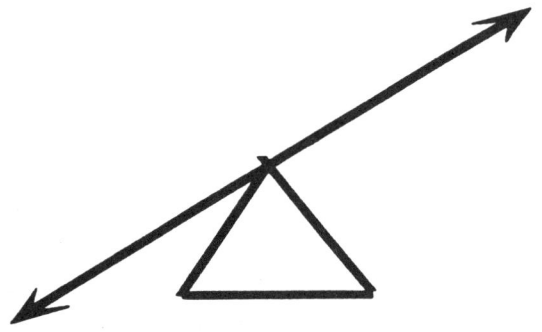

The dog who wouldn't drop briskly.

The dog who wouldn't come briskly, because he might have to drop briskly.

These two situations are interconnected. A dog will initially come briskly, but wouldn't drop quickly. Then, as you start to get a faster response on the drop, the recall slows down. Think of these two situations as ends of a see-saw that you are trying to balance. Eventually, the dog will start to understand and you will get a dog who will come as fast as he can and still drop promptly enough to meet your standards. Some dogs collapse into a down more gracefully and more efficiently than others. Some dogs have better reflexes which enables them to respond faster to a command or signal. You really wouldn't know how fast your dog is capable of reacting until you push him. What can you do to push a dog to drop faster? What follows is a staircase of ideas. As you climb the stairs, the approaches become more severe. Always start at the bottom of the stairs. If a method is going to be effective, you should see and encouraging sign of change after the second time you do it. Don't keep doing things that aren't working.

GETTING A DOG TO DROP!

MOST SEVERE – WORK YOUR
WAY UP ONE STEP AT A TIME !

In rare and extreme cases you might need to resort to an electronic shock collar (start setting on low). 'Make sure the dog is on a long line when starting this. Command "Down" and push the bottom for a brief second.

Tie the dog on a long line to a fence. Measure the line. Command "Down", just before the dog hits end of the line.

Command "Down", and smack a riding crop to the floor! (at your side.)

Command "Down", and squirt the dog in the face with a water gun. Need more? Try a garden hose!

Command "Down", and throw a cup of water into the dog's face.

Throw a chain at the dog.

Command "Down", and throw keys or throw a chain at you feet.

Command, "Down" and throw a toy or a bean bag at the dog's front feet.

Command "Down" and bounce a tennis ball in front of the dog, if he retrieves it, say nothing and put him back in the down.

Command "Down" and thrown a rolled up leash between you and the dog.

Command, "Down" and without moving towards the dog, stomp your foot. (This is more effective indoors where there will be a vibration).

After you command, "Down" step into the dog and bring your palm down on the dog's muzzle. This should be more of a jolt than a push.

After you command, "Down", step into the dog, who should only be about 8 ft. from you and bring your right hand down onto the dog's shoulders as you push down and back.

MILDEST –
START HERE!

GETTING A DOG TO COME!
IF THE DOG WOULDN'T COME WHEN CALLED AFTER HE HAS BEEN TAUGHT TO COME!

PONDER:

> Suppose you have a dog who used to do a good, brisk recall but, since you've enforced a drop, the dog will no longer come to you because he's afraid he might have to drop.

We know that we can always put a dog back on a long line or flexi-leash and force him to come but when the line comes off it will again be his decision. We prefer to encourage him to come (assuming he knew the exercise and is resisting because of the drop) while off leash. The amount of force used should escalate slowly. Always use the mildest correction <u>that works!</u>

Come...Cont'.

SEVERE

Try each step at least twice without results before moving up a step.

- If the dog still isn't coming when called, put him on a long line and once he's responding, go back to the mild end of the staircase. Start the line on a buckle collar and go to a prong if necessary.
- Walk slowly towards the dog. Take hold of both ears at the base of the ear, one in each hand. Lift the dog off his front feet and bring him to you by his ears. SMILE! Praise when he gets to you.
- With a prong collar on the dog, take hold of the fur and skin on top of his head with one hand. Lift the dog onto his hind legs by the fur. As you bring him to you, jerk towards you with the prong collar. Praise when he gets to you.
- Put a prong collar on the dog. Walk slowly towards the dog without eye contact. Lift the dog on the prong collar so he is on his hind legs. Bring him to you on his hind legs. Praise when he gets to you.
- Walk slowly towards the dog with eye contact. With one hand take hold of the fur and skin on top of his head, with your other hand take hold of one of his ears (assuming they are the long furry kind). Bring the dog to you on his hind legs. Praise when you stop.
- Walk slowly towards the dog without eye contact and with both hands take hold of the fur and skin** on the top of the dog's head. Lift the dog so his front feet are just barely off the ground as you bring him into you. Then praise when you stop.
- Walk slowly towards the dog without eye contact and take hold of the fur and skin on top of his head with one hand and the buckle collar with the other. Bring the dog on his hind legs all the way towards you, then praise him.
- Walk slowly toward the dog without eye contact and lift the dog on the buckle collar as you bring him to you on his hind legs.
- Walk slowly towards the dog without eye contact and with the buckle collar lift up as you bring the dog to you and then praise him.
- For the dog who doesn't come, go towards him slowly without making eye contact and with a buckle collar guide him to you and then Praise him. *

MILD

* We avoid eye contact to make the correction less personal and thus milder. We use eye contact to intimidate and thus increase the level of correction.

** Whiskers work well if your dog has them!

Understanding The Broad Jump

Multiple Choice: (Circle all that apply.)

I. In teaching the broad jump exercise we want to impress upon the dog:

    a. That the higher he jumps, the easier it will be for him to clear the broad jump.
    b. That he must get back into a sit front as quickly as possible.
    c. That he must jump from before the first board to beyond the last board in a straight line.

II. Most dogs cut the corner of the broad jump and don't jump straight across because:

    a. It's easier to jump that way.
    b. They are sloppy working dogs.
    c. They are trying to please their trainers by returning to front as quickly as possible.

III. To teach a dog not to step in between the broad jump boards you should:

    a. Start teaching the broad jump with two boards and a bar jump over it.
    b. Keep the boards very close together in the beginning.
    c. Encourage the dog to make the mistake of stepping in between the boards and then put chicken wire down to explain to him that he shouldn't step there.
    d. Put the four (4) boards all up on end.

IV. To teach a dog not to cut the corner of the broad jump you should do all of the following except:

    a. Make sure you taught the dog to turn and sit off the broad jump by putting up a gate (barrier) to direct the dog straight after he jumps.
    b. Refocus the dog's attention by pointing to a spot on the floor past the last board in the middle of jump, just before you send the dog.
    c. Put a toy just beyond the spot where you want the dog to land. If he picks up the toy and brings it to you, accept it and then eventually remove the toy and just point to the spot.
    d. As the dog is in mid-air lift your foot up into the corner where the dog usually cuts. Surprise him with your accuracy!
    e. Put a leash on the dog, run by the jump with the dog and after the dog jumps snap him to you.

(Check the back of this Workbook, for the correct responses.)

GLOVES

I.
Remembering that your back is to the gloves, number the gloves below 1, 2 & 3 the way they would be in the ring.

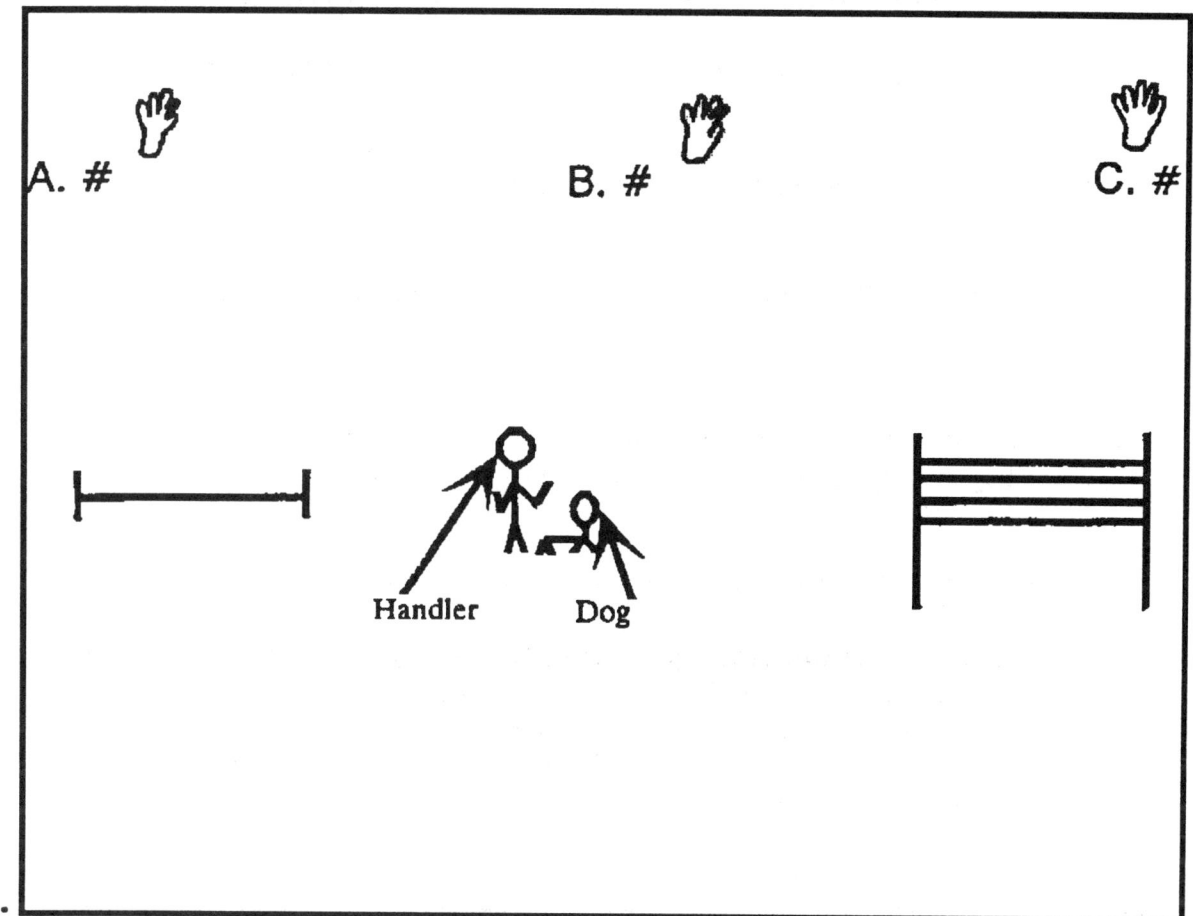

II.
If we pivot to the right to gloves one and two, why do we pivot left to glove number three?

III.
By turning to one glove, but sending the dog to a different glove, we are proofing the dog in case: (Circle all that apply.)

    A. a dog guesses at gloves
    B. a dog makes a bad pivot
    C. a dog always wants glove # 2
    D. a steward puts the glove in the wrong place.

Gloves.... (cont.)

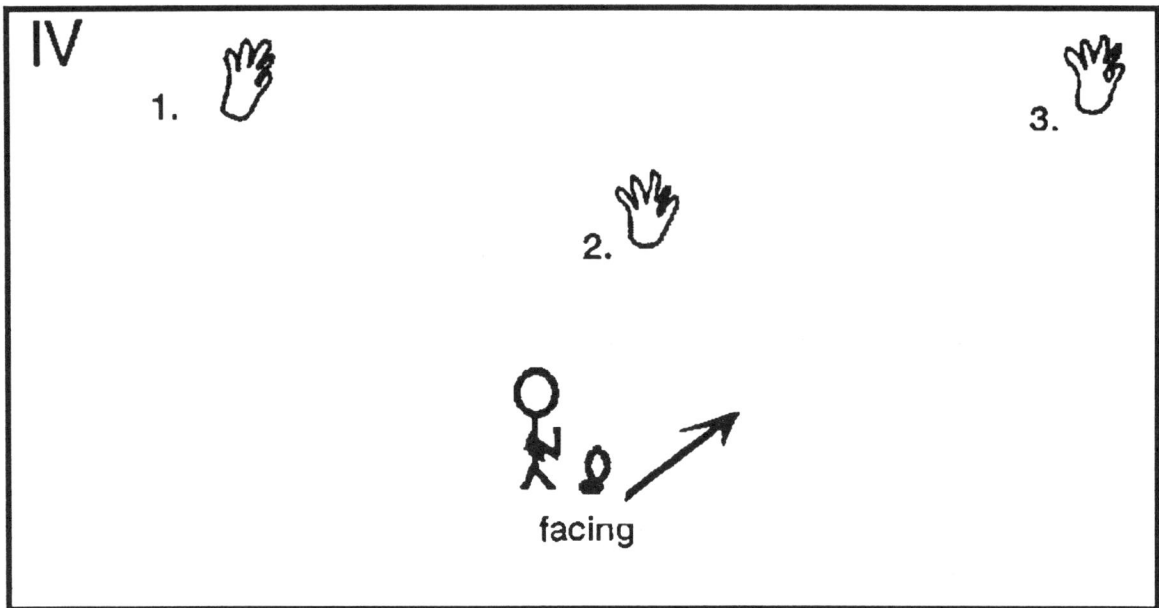

In the setup of gloves pictured above, the center glove is moved closer to the dog & handler to teach the dog:

- A. to retrieve glove # 2
- B. never to retrieve glove #2
- C. to retrieve the glove he is directed to and not the one he sees first
- D. not to get confused between glove # 2 and the other gloves

V. When giving a clear glove signal the top of your left thumb should be even with the bottom of the dog's_____

- A. head
- B. eye
- C. nose
- D. ear

VI. When giving a clear glove signal where a dog can determine a direction, you should say the verbal command, "Take it":

- A. as soon as the hand signal stops moving
- B. as the hand signal moves
- C. before the hand signal is given
- D. not at all

(Check the back of this Workbook, for the correct responses.)

PIVOT LEFT

On page 185 of <u>Beyond Basic Dog Training</u> (Revised Edition) you learn to pivot let with the aid of a dowel.

An alternative method to teaching the pivot left on the command "back" is to attach a second leash around the flank of the dog. Bring the leash attached to the dog's rear behind your back and hold it in your right hand. Your left hand holds the leash attached to the dog's collar. As you bring your right foot directly in front of the dog's front left paw and command "Back" or "Off", pull up slightly with your left hand and with your right hand pull the dog's rump in the direction of your left leg. Some dogs prefer to be pulled by a leash rather than tapped with a stick. While the end result is the same, we are always searching for the method that is the least stressful for the dog.

SCENT ARTICLE PROBLEMS

ASK YOURSELF ???

And get the Ball rolling

OOOOOOOOOOOO

SCENT ARTICLES SCENARIO – – –

I was in a sit, looking ahead as someone laid out my leather and metal "dumbbells". My owner then had me sit at heel with our backs to the pile. I noticed she was holding a dumbbell and smiling down at me as the judge chatted with her. I continued to pay attention to her. Then she handed him the dumbbell and he disappeared behind us. I heard him speak to her. She then brought her right hand across her body to my nose, and back to her side. I knew this meant we were about to do scent articles. She told me to "Heel" and we executed an about turn, my eyes on "Heel" position all the while. Then she said, "Find It" and I immediately raced out to the pile and began sniffing. As is my "pattern" I started at the top of the pile (my owner calls it 12 O'Clock) and worked to the right or "Clockwise". As I smell, I find a stranger's smell on most of the dumbbells and I keep checking until I come to my owner's. *Even though I haven't smelled all the dumbbells, I know which one smells like my owner and I trot confidently back to her. She is standing perfectly still, looking straight ahead, with a pleasant look on her face. I sit front, being sure to line up my nose and body with my "Front Point". I would like to roll the dumbbell to the back of my mouth, but I know I shouldn't, so I resist the urge. My owner takes the dumbbell from my mouth, saying "Give". I know what comes next and I await her "Heel" command excitedly. I hear the command, "Heel" and I briskly go around behind my trainer, head up, looking for my "Heel" point on her left hip. She releases me, and praises me and we once again we set up with our backs to the pile. Guess What? I get to do this again !

How would you score this dog?

* I notice that there are a lot of good smells in the grass and in the air, but I am not allowed to sniff anything but my dumbbell.

HIDDEN PICTURES

1) Set a timer to three (3) minutes.

2) By studying the picture below, see if in three (3) minutes you can find:

       10 Scent articles.
       1 Pair of tongues for putting out articles.
       1 Scent article case.
       1 Tie–down board for teaching scent articles.

READY ?　　➤➤➤➤➤➤　　START!

Hidden....Cont'.

How many items did you miss?

Did you feel pressured by the time limit?

Look at the answers at the back of this workbook, for the correct response.

Does it now look obvious to you?

Do you think the dog, searching for a scented article in a pile has some of these feelings?

Even though there is no actual time limit for the dog, do you think he senses one?

Why do you think dogs panic while doing articles and then grab anything?

GO – OUTS

The Go – Out is divided into three (3) teaching stages:

    A. Teach the dog to leave your side.
    B. Teach the dog to go until you tell him to stop.
    C. Teach the dog to go in a straight line.

Below are listed different steps in teaching the go–out. See if you can tell which **Stage** or **Stages** each step is teaching.

1. Handler leaves dog and walks out and points to go out. Then handler returns and sends the dog.

    Which Stage? _____

2. Handler puts out three sets of chutes defining go–out.

    Which Stage? _____

3. Dog is on a long line, and following the Go–Out command, is gently pulled away from the handler.

    Which Stage? _____

4. Handler touches the dog's nose gently to the barrier.

    Which Stage? _____

5. Handler sends the dog, but then stops him in the second set of chutes before he reaches the barrier.

    Which Stage? _____

Go–Outs...Cont.

6. Handler tells the dog to stay and throws a ball into the corner of the ring. Then handler commands, "Go–Out" to the dog.

    Which Stage? _____

7. Handler does go–outs to different barriers.

    Which Stage? _____

8. Handler commands "Go–Out" but the dog only goes four (4) steps and stops. Handler takes the dog out to go out by holding the collar in his left hand, from behind the dogs head, and pushes the dog ahead of himself. This helps to assure that the dog does not think he is heeling.

    Which Stage? _____

9. Handler starts to wean the dog off the chutes by making them smaller in size and by pulling them back away from the gates.

    Which Stage? _____

(Check the back of this Workbook, for the correct responses.)

GO – OUTS

Picture yourself with your new Utility dog facing "Go–Outs" in preparation to do the directed jumping exercise.

Now think about:

The ever changing sight picture of the go–out makes it a very challenging exercise to perfect. Below is a list of things that could work to pull a dog off center on the go–out. Put a T for true or an F for false next to each item.

THINGS THAT PULL A DOG OFF CENTER ON GO–OUT *

___ 1. Having recently gone to a corner for a glove.
___ 2. A strong wind.
___ 3. Being in a new ring/location.
___ 4. Going to a different background (wall, string barrier)
___ 5. A tree in the distance.
___ 6. Your spouse.
___ 7. Lack of focus or attention on the part of your dog.
___ 8. A magnet.
___ 9. A shadow on the mat.
___ 10. Barriers that are moving due to the wind.
___ 11. Tall grass.
___ 12. A full moon.
___ 13. A dog and handler working in the ring next to you.
___ 14. A hill in the ring.

*What can you do to teach the dog to work past the distractions?

(Check the back of this Workbook, for the correct responses.)

UNDERSTANDING PROOFING

Proofing is a technique used to test the dog's understanding of an exercise.

Proofs may be:
- **A** uditory (what the dog hears)
- **V** isual (what the dog sees)
- **O** lfactory (what the dog smells), or
- **K** inesthetic (what the dog feels.)

It is important to proof each exercise with all four senses.

Below is a list of proofs. See if you can determine which **sense**, or **senses** are being proofed.

A = Auditory   **V** = Visual   **O** = Olfactory   **K** = Kinesthetic

1. Applause   ___
2. Rain   ___
3. Rattling baby gates   ___
4. Someone petting the dog   ___
5. Bitch in season standing next to the articles.   ___
6. Ball rolling by the dog   ___
7. Person barking like a dog   ___
8. Person offering the dog food   ___
9. Coat hanging off a jump   ___
10. Cookies on the ground near dog   ___
11. Someone gently pulling the dog's collar to get him up off a stay. ___
12. Calling from the corner of the ring to a dog doing go outs.   ___

Proofing....cont.

13. Standing over a dog doing signals. ___
14. Putting a dumbbell up on a step. ___
15. Putting a dumbbell on its end. ___
16. Having someone say down in the middle of a recall to proof a drop on recall. ___
17. A strange dog walking in front of a dog on a stay. ___
18. The handler giving signals while kneeling on the ground. ___
19. Looking at one jump in directed jumping and signaling the dog to the other jump. ___
20. A glove placed in a hole so it's not easily seen by the dog. ___

TRY THIS:

Take eight different proofs, two from each sense and try them on your dog. See if you can tell which sense of his is most likely to cause a distraction. Do you have the kind of dog who sees everything or one who notices every smell? Once you know your dog's weakness you can tailor your proofing.

(Check the back of this Workbook, for the correct responses.)

MISTAKES DOGS MAKE

The more dogs you train through Novice, Open and Utility, the more you realize that at each level of training, dogs of all breeds seem to make similar mistakes. The same confusions, anticipations and exercises in which the dog may be easily distracted, are found repeatedly in training. The experienced trainer has the advantage of almost being able to **predict** where the dog will make mistakes. These are viewed as learning stages and the experienced trainer is pleased to see that the dog has progressed to this level of confusion.

Knowing that certain mistakes are inevitable, the experienced trainer works to cause confusion in training and to then train beyond it. The inexperienced trainer prays that the dog will somehow continue to perform the exercise correctly and enters the dog in a show only to find out that the dog is confused about something he "always does right at home."

Causing a Mistake

In order to fix a problem you must be able to cause the problem in training. Some dogs willingly make the same mistakes in training that they do in the ring. For other dogs, the trainer must be creative enough to cause the mistake in training. If you have been known to say, "he only does it in the ring" then you are not trying hard enough to cause the mistake in practice. Could it be because you want him to be right so badly?

Below is a list of training problems.
See how many you can figure out how to cause.

1) In a ring the dog lies down on the sit stay. In practice he does the sit stay. How would you cause him to lie down?

2) In a ring the dog takes forever to get around on the finish and he usually ends up wide. In practice he comes around close and briskly. How can you cause the slow finish in training?

3) In the ring the dog goes around the high jump. In practice he always goes over it. How can you cause him to go around the high jump?

4) In the ring the dog gets up and follows you when you leave him for a recall. In practice he always waits to be called. How can you cause him to anticipate the recall?

5) In the ring the dog left on a stand signal in Utility, follows you by taking steps after the stay signal. In practice the dog stands like a rock. How can you cause the walking in practice?

6) In the ring the dog stops short on the go-out. In practice, he always goes to the end of the ring. How can you cause a short go-out in practice?

****

Think of a problem not listed here which your dog only does in a ring:

_____
_____
_____
_____
_____

Now be creative and think about how you might cause it in practice:

_____
_____
_____
_____

(Check the answers at the back of this Workbook, for the correct responses.)

Mistakes.....cont.

Below are lists of mistakes most dogs make in Novice, Open and Utility. Put a line through each one your dog has already experienced and learned to avoid.

NOVICE:

1. The dog ends up on your right side after an about turn on heeling.
2. The dog stands and starts coming towards you as you cross the ring to do a recall.
3. The dog anticipates the finish command and goes directly to heel position.
4. The dog sits as you return to heel position on the stand for exam.
5. The dog goes down on the Long—Sit.
6. The dog gets up on the Long—Down.
7. The dog while heeling gets distracted and lags.
8. The dog, interested in the judge examining him, turns his head and walks a few steps on the stand for exam.
9. The dog is distracted and doesn't notice that you have halted. He forges ahead or circles around behind you.
10. The dog sniffs the ground on the Long—Down and ends up crawling out of position.
11. The dog gets up to start heeling before you take the first step. (anticipation)
12. The dog runs past you on a recall and doesn't sit front.
13. The dog does not move on your command to finish.

Mistakes... Cont.

OPEN:

1. The dog anticipates the drop on recall, in the middle of the recall.
2. As the handler calls the dog to come on the drop on recall, the dog stands up and drops immediately.
3. The dog can't find the dumbbell you threw, and gives up.
4. The dog goes around the high jump on the way out.
5. The dog goes over the jump, picks up the dumbbell, comes back around the jump.
6. The dog walks through the boards of the broad jump.
7. The dog jumps to the handler on the broad jump, thus cutting the corner.
8. On the retrieve on flat the dog comes back over the high jump.
9. The dog goes down on the Long-sit out of sight.
10. The dog swivels out of position on the Long-sit so he can see where the handler went out of sight.
11. The dog gets up on the long down out of sight.
12. The dog freezes on the heel off leash.
13. The dog anticipates a finish and goes directly to heel.
14. The dog lands off the broad jump and makes a wide turn before returning to the handler.
15. The dog picks up the dumbbell and hesitates (distraction) before returning with it.
16. The dog touches (crashes) the handler when doing fronts or presenting the dumbbell.
17. The dog anticipates the second half of the drop on recall and comes before being called.
18. The handler calls the dog and commands "down" and the dog doesn't drop
19. The dog runs past the dumbbell before picking it up.

Mistakes.....Cont.

UTILITY:

1. The dog is distracted on signals and doesn't drop when you give the signal.

2. The dog drops but is nervous about being so far away from you, so he flinches when you give a sit signal but doesn't come totally up into a sit.

3. The dog goes directly to heel on signals, confusing it with the stand for exam in motion.

4. When you send the dog to do articles, the dog is disoriented and does a go out instead.

5. You give a directed jumping signal and the dog confuses it with signals — and drops.

6. On a go-out the dog lies down instead of sitting.

7. On a go-out the dog goes out over a jump.

8. You pivot and send to glove #1 or #3 and the dog retrieves glove #2.

9. The dog retrieves the glove and comes back to you over a jump.

10. The dog stops short on a go-out, before you say "Sit."

11. The dog panics when he can't find the scented article, grabs the wrong one, and comes in to you.

Mistakes....Cont.

12. The dog comes over a jump and fronts to the judge.
13. The dog doesn't wait to see your signal and comes over the wrong jump. (Often does the first jump correctly and then just takes the same jump again.)
14. The dog anticipates the moving stand.
15. The dog comes front instead of to heel on moving stand.
16. The dog does a go-out into the corner where he retrieved the glove.
17. The dog picks up the glove and tries to kill it.
18. The dog goes out to the articles, picks up the correct article starts to come back, and freezes.
19. The dog goes out to the article pile and sniffs the grass in between the articles.
20. The dog heads for the correct glove and switches midstream to take a wrong glove that he just noticed.
21. After you say "sit" on the Go-Out, the dog walks towards you a few steps before sitting.

Having crossed out each mistake your dog has already made and learned to avoid, you should be left with mistakes that are likely to happen. You need to cause them in training when you are in control and then work to explain to the dog why they are incorrect.

ASK YOURSELF:

How can I proof and cause each of these errors?

GETTING TO THE ROOT OF THE PROBLEM!

When an obedience exercise is not done perfectly, it is important that the trainer knows exactly what part of the exercise is weak. When the trainer focuses in on the exact weak link in the exercise, then the practice can be put in the place where it will be most effective. It is not beneficial for a dog to repeat a complete exercise over and over again just to improve on one small part. Sometimes such unnecessary repetition causes new problems and a poor work attitude.

Root of the Problem....Cont.

What is the weak link?

1. The dog goes out to the article pile sniffs one or two articles and then stands over the pile doing nothing.   What is the weak link?

    a. The dog works too slowly.
    b. The dog is not paying attention.
    c. The dog has a weak retrieve.
    d. The articles came untied too soon.

2. The dog does a brisk recall and touches the handler as he comes in and ends up sitting crooked.   What is the weak link?

    a. The dog needs work timing fronts.
    b. The dog needs to pay better attention.
    c. The dog needs to learn to slow down.
    d. The dog doesn't understand recall.

3. The dog lags on heeling .   What is the weak link?

    a. The dog needs motivation.
    b. The dog needs to learn to pay attention.
    c. The dog needs to learn where heel position is.
    d. The handler needs to learn a correct pace.

4. The dog swings wide after doing a broad jump.
     What is the weak link?

    a. The dog needs to go back and re-learn how to jump a broad jump.
    b. The dog needs to know what to do after he lands off of a broad jump.
    c. The dog needs to be more motivated to come to the handler.
    d. All of the above.

5. The dog lags on the outside of the figure eight (8).
     What is the weak link?

    a. The dog needs to learn how to bend his body and push with his rear to keep up on the outside turn.
    b. The handler needs to slow down on the outside of the figure 8.
    c. The dog needs to learn to pay attention.
    d. The dog needs to learn where heel position is.

(Check the back of this Workbook, for the correct responses.)

MYSTERY STORIES!

Below are two mystery stories.
Each contains enough clues to solve the mystery.
O. K. Sherlock Bones,
see if you can find the clues and solve the puzzle.

Case # 1.

Midnight, a black Pomeranian is trained through Utility and has her C.D. She has been polishing her open work for six (6) months and is now ready to show in Open. She has been trained to drop on the recall to hand or voice. Her training of the drop on recall includes all the proofing explained in <u>Beyond Basic Dog Training.</u> (New Updated Edition) Midnight has been to many match shows and has received a qualifying open score many times. In her first Open A Trial, indoors, the black Pomeranian works a beautiful class, but doesn't drop on the drop on recall. She trots in briskly without so much as a hesitation. The big, kind man who was judging, feels very badly at the end of the class. Her trainer works all week proofing the drop. Midnight responds confidently to hand or voice in all kinds of distracting situations. She practices dropping on all kinds of surfaces and in all different parts of the recall. All week long Midnight does her drop on recall easily and in fact, by Thursday, she even anticipates a drop. The following weekend Midnight shows outdoors in Open A under a slim, tall, middle-age female judge. Once again, Midnight works a beautiful class and doesn't even think about the possibility of dropping on the recall. It's as if there never was a signal.

Why doesn't Midnight drop in a trial?

For Clue see page: 70

For Answer see page: 166

MYSTERY STORIES!

O. K. Sherlock Bones,
see if you can find the clues and solve the puzzle.

Case # 2.

A golden retriever continually cuts the broad jump in shows.

During practice and correction matches, the owner stands close to the boards in case she needs to stick out her foot while the dog is in mid-air. The strange thing is, the dog never cuts the corner in practice nor in correction matches.

Why does this dog only cut in the broad jump in trials?

For Clue see page: 70

For Answer see page: 166

MYSTERY STORIES!

O. K. Sherlock Bones,
see if you can find the clues and solve the puzzle.

Case # 3.

A handler takes her new U.D. dog out to train. They go to the front yard and she sets the dog up to do a recall at one end of the Utility ring. The handler turns around, and calls the dog in a clear, happy tone of voice. The dog flinches, thinking that perhaps the dog didn't hear her, the handler calls again. Again, the dog looks as if she wants to come, but doesn't.
to come, but doesn't.

Why is this dog not coming?

For Clue see page: 70

For Answer see page: 166

MYSTERY STORIES CLUES !!

Case # 1.

    Clue: Midnight is a very small dog.

Case # 2.

    Clue: When this first began occurring, the solution that worked was touching the dog in mid-air. After one bump, this dog responded by not landing by the corner.

Case # 3.

    Clue: The dog is at the end of a Utility ring.

THE "W" LEARNING CURVE

When you arrive at a problem or a learning stage in training there is a pattern of learning that is often observed. I think of this as " W " learning curve because of you were to graph the dog's progress, it would end up looking like the letter. " W ".

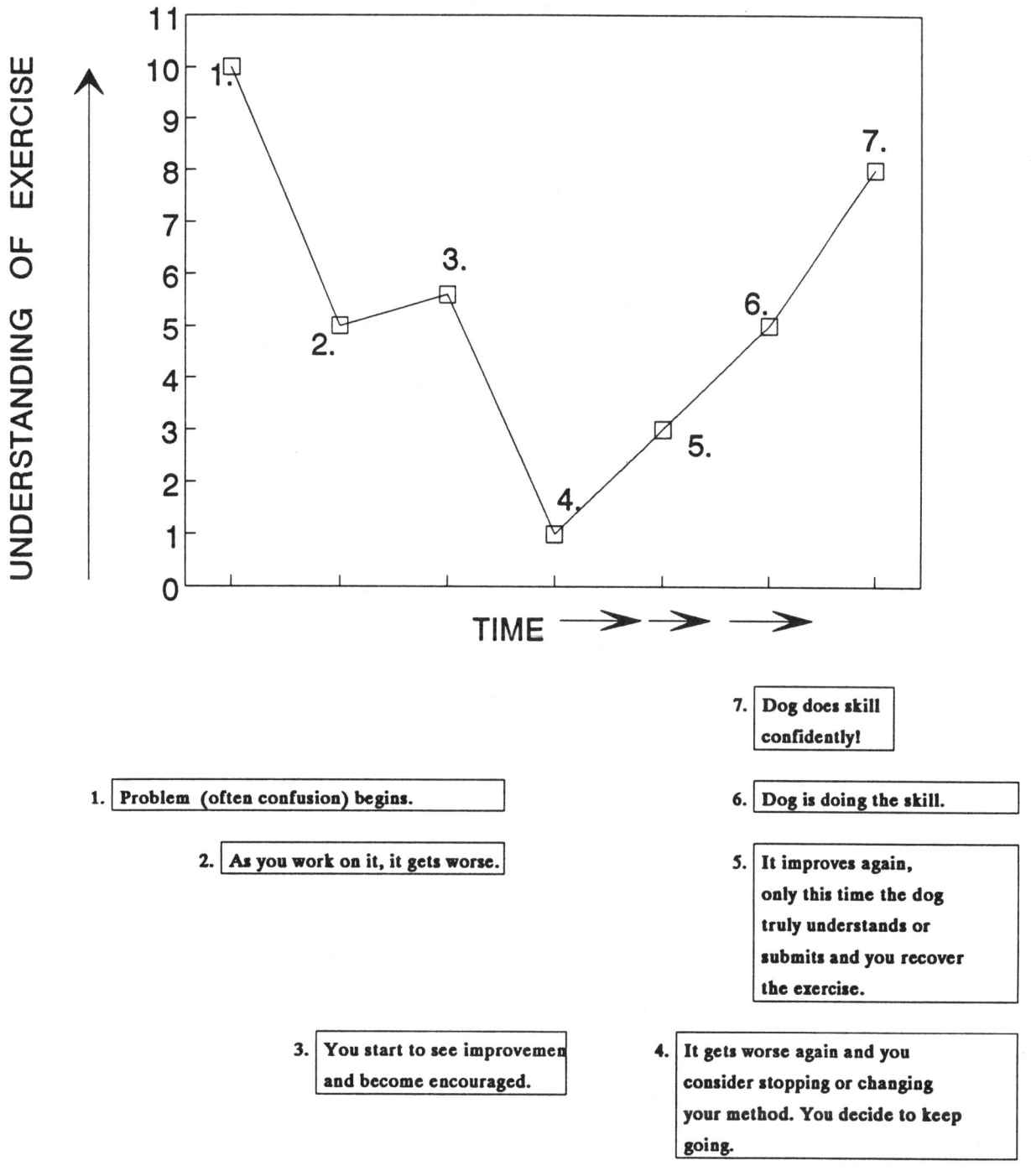

1. Problem (often confusion) begins.
2. As you work on it, it gets worse.
3. You start to see improvemen and become encouraged.
4. It gets worse again and you consider stopping or changing your method. You decide to keep going.
5. It improves again, only this time the dog truly understands or submits and you recover the exercise.
6. Dog is doing the skill.
7. Dog does skill confidently!

"W" CURVE... (cont.)

Let's look at a practical example of the "W" learning curve.

Jane is training a dog who has learned a recall and the down in motion. For a week now Jane has been putting the drop into the formal recall. She has been dropping the dog about 12 feet in front of herself and walking in immediately following the signal. For four days the dog has been coming briskly and dropping promptly. The fifth day, Jane calls the dog and the dog gets up and drops on its own.

Put an "A" on the "W" learning curve where Jane is now!

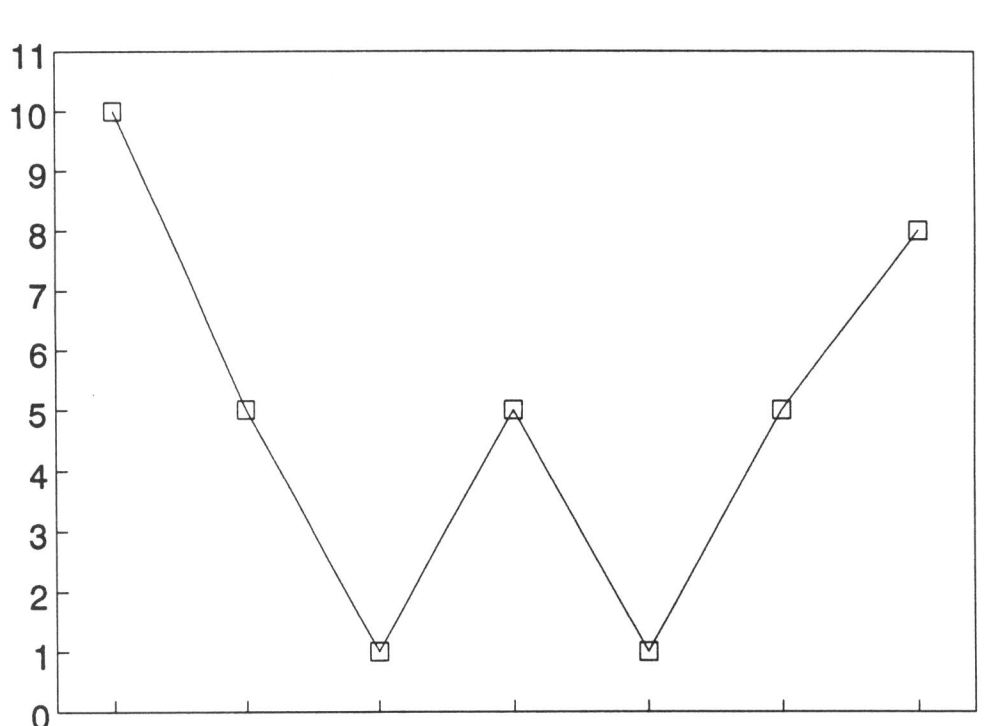

See Answers Page   167

"W" CURVE... (cont.)

Jane is not surprised that the dog anticipated the drop and she knows what to do. Jane calmly walks towards the dog without making eye contact and gently brings him to her. On the next recall, Jane calls and the dog doesn't move. Jane understands that this is because the dog is confused and rather than make another error, the dog does nothing. Again Jane walks towards the dog and gently brings him to her. On the next recall the dog gets up and drops immediately. Since the dog has changed his behavior each time there is no reason for Jane to escalate the correction, and so once again she walks calmly to the dog without eye contact and gently brings him to her. On the next attempt the dog comes in on the recall slowly. Jane can see that the dog is thinking about dropping but doesn't. Jane calls the dog again on a straight recall and this time the dog is almost up to a brisk trot.

Put a "B" where Jane is now on the " W " learning curve!

II

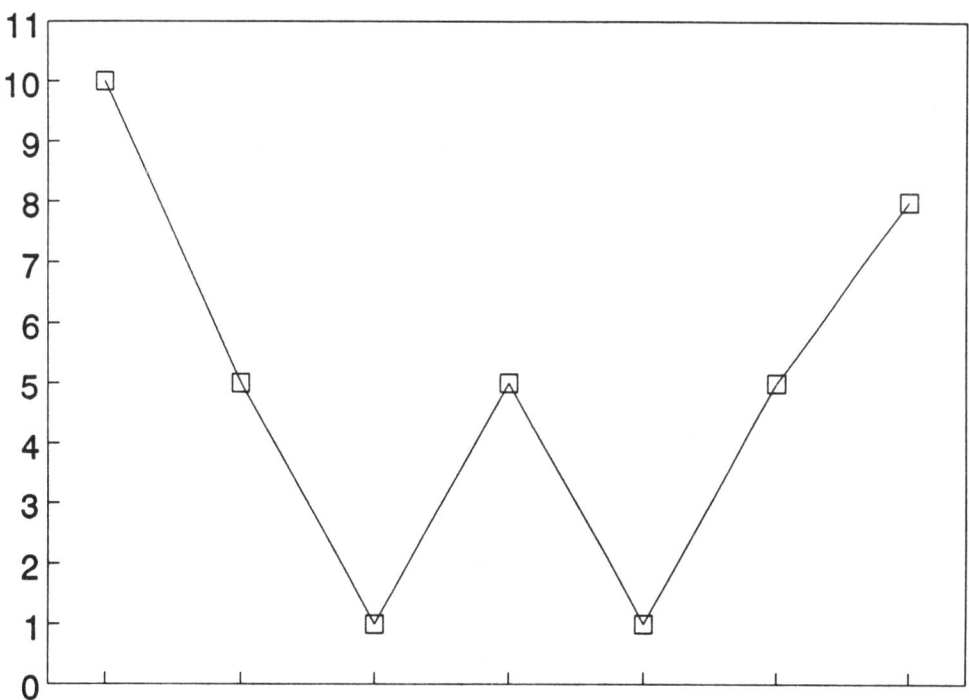

See Answers Page   167

" W " CURVE... (cont.)

Having gotten the dog doing a recall, Jane now calls the dog and drops him. The dog drops willingly. The next time Jane calls the dog, he gets up, trots 5 steps and anticipates the drop.

Put a "C" where Jane is now on the " W " curve!

III

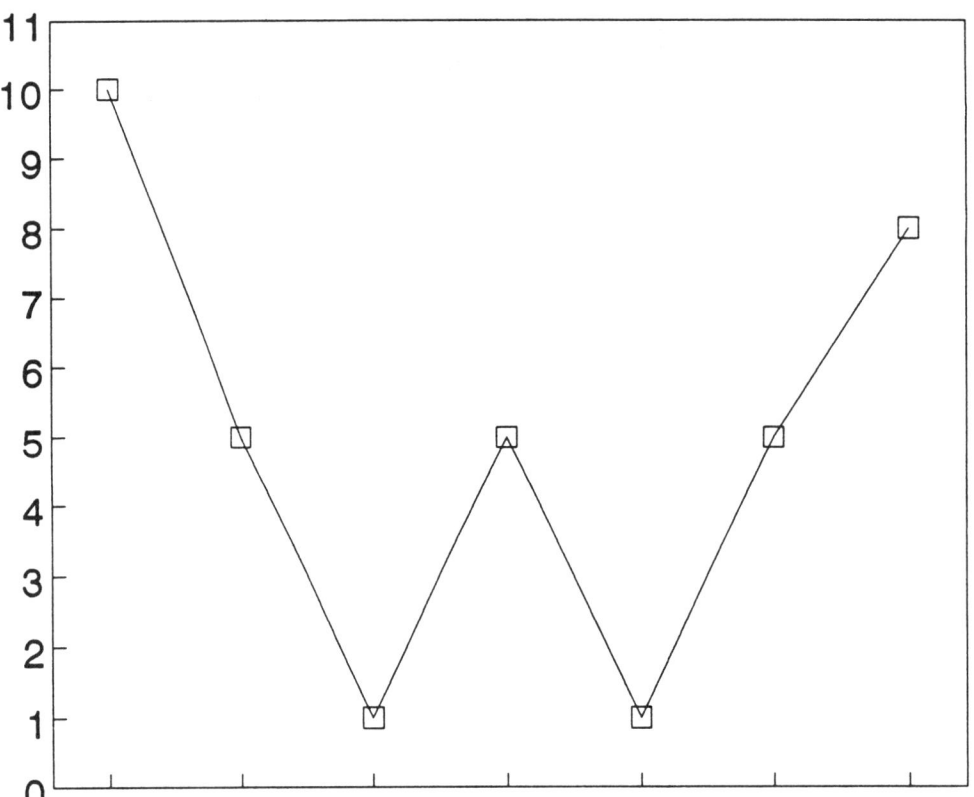

See Answers Page   162

" W " CURVE... (cont.)

On the next recall, the dog again anticipates by dropping before he is asked to. Jane gently guides the dog into front and by the following recall the dog is back to trotting in. With the recall back, Jane drops the dog on the next recall. The dog drops willingly. Now is the real test. In the past, following a drop, the dog has either anticipated or not come at all. Jane calls her dog. The dog gets up and moves towards her slowly. Jane does nothing to encourage speed because she knows that confidence on the part of the dog will bring back the speed on the recall and if she intervenes now, the dog will rely on her to tell him when he should move quickly because there is not going to be a drop. Even though the dog is coming in slowly, when he gets 10 ft. from her, Jane signals the dog to drop. Relieved, the dog collapses. Jane knows that occasionally you must drop a dog who is coming in slowly because if you don't, the dog will realize that if he creeps in sheepishly, his trainer will never drop him! As Jane repeats the exercise the recall speed increases slightly.

Put a "D" where Jane is now on the " W " curve!

IV

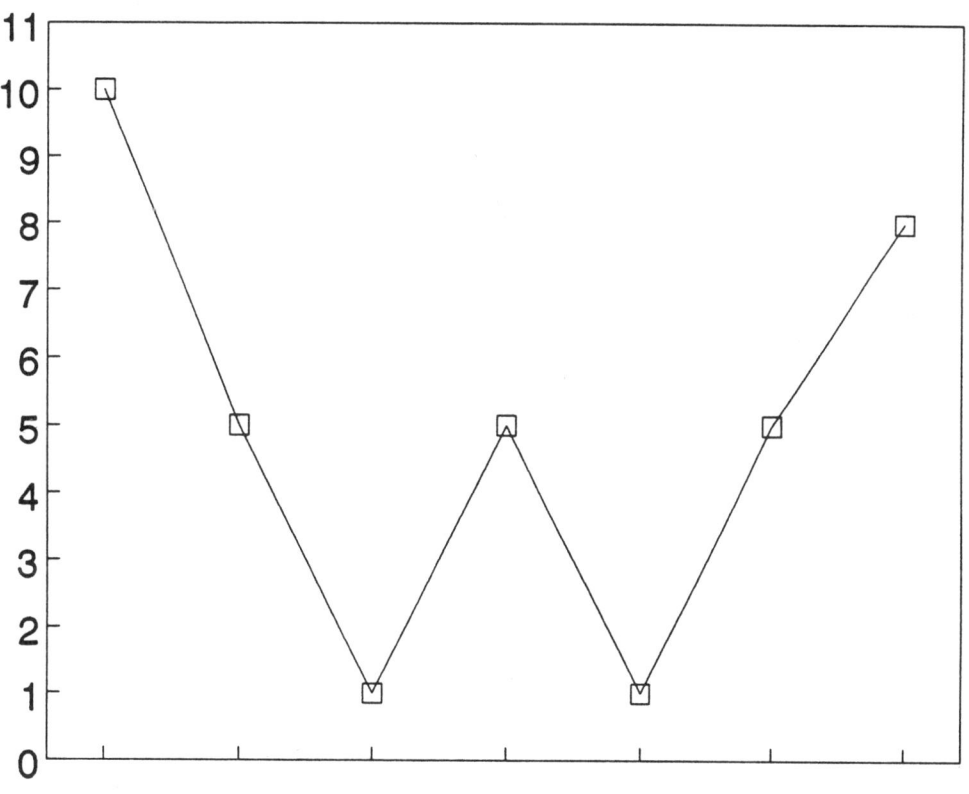

See Answers Page ___167___

" W " CURVE... (cont.)

Where will Jane be in the learning curve the next time Jane goes out to work the dog?   This will depend on the dog Jane is training.

It is possible that she will go through the entire " W " again in the next training session. Actually, with the drop on recall exercise, dogs take anywhere from 3 – 8 weeks before they illustrate real understanding of the exercise.

Regardless of the exercise, the " W " learning curve helps us remember that things often get worse, before they eventually get better.

(Check the back of this Workbook, for the correct responses.)

SOLVING TRAINING PROBLEMS
ANALYZING YOUR DOG'S BEHAVIOR

DATE: _____ TIME: _____ LOCATION: _____

1. What is the dog doing wrong?

2. This behavior is: (circle one)

    a. a problem   b.   a learning stage

(A **problem** is a mistake that only a few dogs make. For example, a dog who avoids picking up a metal article.

A **learning stage** is a mistake that most dogs make in the learning process. For example, a dog who anticipates a drop on recall is in a learning stage.)

3. Why is the dog behaving in this manner? Is he: (circle one)

    a. confused?
    b. afraid?
    c. distracted?
    d. feels he has a choice?

4. What did you observe that helped you answer question #3?

5. Your response should be to: (circle one)

    a. help the dog
    b. correct the dog

Training Problems.....Cont'.

6. Complete the chart below to explain the techniques you would use at three different levels of help or correction.

	HELP	CORRECTION
1. I would:		
2. If that didn't work, I would:		
3. If I still got no results, I would:		

SOLVING TRAINING PROBLEMS ANALYZING YOUR BEHAVIOR WHILE TRAINING

DATE:_____ TIME:_____ LOCATION:_____

1. What exercise were you working on?

2. What did the dog do or not do?

3. Has the dog ever done this before? If so, how long ago and how many times?

4. How long had you been training the dog in this session when the behavior occurred?

5. Did you look at the situation from the dog's point of view? If so, what did you see?

6. What was your physical (training) reaction to the dog's behavior?

7. What was your emotional reaction to the dog's behavior?

8. How did you approach the problem? (Planning to help or correct?)

9. How long did you train before you were able to effect some change in the dog's behavior?

10. Did you refer to the textbook <u>Beyond Basic Dog Training</u> to reread the appropriate pages?

11. Did you at any time feel yourself losing patience? If so, what did you do to regain control?

12. How will you handle the problem the next time the behavior occurs?

13. How did you end the training session?

14. What was the dog's mental state of mind at the end of the training session?

15. How did you feel at the end of the training session?

THE GAP

Why do dogs perform better in training than they do in the obedience ring?
Where is "THE GAP" between training and showing?

DIRECTIONS:
Decide where the following events take place and put a wherever it applies.

	EVENTS	DURING TRAINING	WHILE SHOWING
1	Crowded, noisy, smelly distractions.		
2	Use of prong collar.		
3	Nervous handler, distracted, stiff, walking slower than normal.		
4	Confident handler walking with brisk pace.		
5	Handler giving abundant praise throughout the exercise.		
6	No corrections or praise during the exercise.		
7	Corrections for all minor mistakes.		
8	Use of direct eye contact (hard eyes) while heeling.		
9	Use of peripheral vision while heeling, (soft eyes).		
10	Direct eye contact during signal exercise.		
11	Soft eye contact during signal exercise so the handler can see the judge's signals.		
12	Small brief work sessions with periods of play.		
13	A long drive in the car before the work session.		
14	Being crated or confined before the work session.		
15	Unfamiliar looking jumps.		
16	Handler calm enough to think about footwork.		
17	An unknown person issuing commands and carrying a clipboard.		
18	A loud speaker in the background.		
19	A person standing and/or walking behind a dog as the dog comes in for a recall.		
20	Praise only at completion of the exercise.		
21	Dog is under control in between exercises.		
22	Strange person measures dog before heeling begins.		
23	The heeling pattern is short requiring many transitions in a small amount of space.		
24	Dog sees a ring barrier for Go-Outs.		
25	Dog does Go-Outs to a crowd of people.		

THE GAP... (cont)

Ideally, the experience of training should resemble the experience of showing if the dog is to perform as well as he does in practice.   If your training does not reflect show conditions, or if your behavior as a handler changes when showing, your dog will be unprepared for the obedience ring.

Look at the checks you have put in the two columns. If you put a check   (✓) under showing but not training, ask yourself:

     1. How can I set up the same situation in training?
            OR
     2. How can I remove this situation from showing?

If you put a check   (✓)   under training, but not showing, ask yourself:

     1. Is my dog becoming dependent on this to the point where I see a lesser performance without it?

     2. Can I do these things at a match show and then wean the dog off of them slowly?

As you get checks in both boxes or no checks in either box for these events, you will start to remove   THE GAP between training and showing!

Planning To Show at a Match Show?

Put an (X) in all that apply.

I am going to a:

1. ☐ "Show N Go" or fun match where I can freely correct and/or help my dog.
2. ☐ A sanctioned OB match where I know the judge and he or she will let me make reasonable corrections.
3. ☐ A sanctioned OB match where I don't know the judge.
4. ☐ A sanctioned OA match where I know the judge and he or she will let me help the dog through the exercises.
5. ☐ A sanctioned OA match where I don't know the judge.

If you put a (X) in number 5, cancel your plans and stay home. You will gain nothing showing your dog at a match where you can't correct or help your dog. See Chapter 49 of <u>Beyond Basic Dog Training</u>

My main goal for going to this match show is:

1. ☐ To see how much my dog's performance changes when I'm around show conditions (distractions)
2. ☐ To correct a problem that is likely to occur in a ring situation but only happens in practice when I force it to happen. (example: dog who does not respond to the Down Signal in Utility under the stress of a ring but does it readily at home in practice.)
3. ☐ To test my handling under show-like conditions.
4. ☐ To get away from my spouse, work and/or children.
5. ☐ Not to enter my dog but to train my dog in a show-like atmosphere.
6. ☐ To test to see how my dog and I would have scored if we were at a Trial.
7. ☐ To build my dog's confidence in the ring.

At most Match Shows, if you show FEO (for exhibition only) you may enter your dog more than one time. It is to your advantage not to work on more than one goal each time you go into the ring. Except for goal #4, select one goal for each entry and work towards that goal.

For example, if you are working on goals 1, 3, 6 or 7, you will plan not to correct or help the dog as much as if you were working on goals 7 or 2. If goal 7 (building confidence) is your objective then you might plan to verbally encourage the dog or put out 'go-out' guides, or even point out front and finish points to focus on.

MATCH SHOWS... (cont.)

Your dog's first few match-show experiences are very important. They will often determine the feelings a dog has about showing. Make sure the first few match shows are more like helpful, happy training sessions that just happen to occur in a ring. As the dog gains ring experience and confidence, you can slowly back off the verbal and physical help. Some dogs suffer from "stage fright" and will need help for many match shows before they can perform in public.

Keep track of your match show experiences by filling out the Match Show log at the back of this workbook.

SAMPLE
MATCH SHOW LOG

Name of Match/Show: _____
Date: _____
Location (I/O): _____
Weather: _____
Ring Conditions: _____
Judge: _____
Class: _____
Your Goal: _____

Things dog did well: _____

that surprised you?: _____

Not Perfect Yet: _____

Score (if any): [   ]

⚜ Why did the dog lose points?
⚜ Did you notice your need for more proofing?
⚜ Did you correct at a Match?
⚜ Were there unusual conditions?

Leg or Title?: [   ]

Score Breakdown

Exercise	Max Score	Your Score	Comments
TOTAL:			

MATCH SHOWS/Show log... (cont.)

Was this the dog's first, second, third, etc..... class of the day? –

What did you learn from this experience?:
_____
_____
_____
_____
_____
_____
_____
_____

HOW DID YOU FEEL IN THE RING?

(circle all that apply)

        Rhythmical

        In Control

        Nervous

        Excited

        Relaxed

        Focused

        Forgot Footwork

        Did more than my job

        Out of Rhythm

        Moved too slow

        Moved too fast

OBEDIENCE TRIAL CHAMPIONSHIP

Championship points will be recorded only for those dogs which have earned the Utility Dog Title. Any dog that has been awarded the title of Obedience Trial Champion may continue to complete, and if such dog earns a First or Second place ribbon, that dog shall also earn the points.

Championship points will be recorded for those dogs which have earned a First or Second place ribbon competing in the Open B or Utility Class (or Utility B, if divided), according to the schedule of points established by the Board of Directors of The American Kennel Club. In counting the number of eligible dogs in competition, a dog that is disqualified, or is dismissed, excused or expelled from the ring by the Judge shall not be included.

Requirements for the Obedience Trial Champion are as follows:

1. Shall have won 100 points, and
2. shall have won a First place in Utility (or Utility B, if divided) provided there are at least three dogs in competition; and
3. shall have won a First place in Open B provided there are at least six dogs in competition; and
4. shall have won a third First place under the conditions of 2 or 3 above; and
5. shall have won these three First places under three different Judges, at all breed obedience trials, whether held separately or in conjunction with an all breed dog show.

OBEDIENCE TRIAL CHAMPIONSHIP

POINT SCHEDULE

OPEN B CLASS

NUMBER COMPETING	POINTS FOR FIRST PLACE	POINTS FOR SECOND PLACE
6–10	2	0
11–15	4	1
16–20	6	2
21–25	10	3
26–30	14	4
31–35	18	5
36–40	22	7
41–45	26	9
46–50	30	11
51–56	34	13

UTILITY CLASS

NUMBER COMPETING	POINTS FOR FIRST PLACE	POINTS FOR SECOND PLACE
3–4	2	0
5–7	4	1
8–10	6	2
11–13	10	3
14–16	14	4
17–19	17	5
20–23	20	7
24–26	24	9
27–29	27	11
30–32	30	13
33–36	33	14
37–40	37	15
41 and Over	40	17

SUMMARY OF O.T.CH. POINTS

	DATE	JUDGE	HOST CLUB	CLASS	PLACE	# DOGS	POINTS
Open B — 1st Place							
Utility — 1st Place							
Additional — 1st Place							

TRIAL	DATE	JUDGE	SCORE	CLASS	PLACE	# DOGS	POINTS	TOTALS

O.T.CH. Points...Cont'.

TRIAL	DATE	JUDGE	SCORE	CLASS	PLACE	# DOGS	POINTS	TOTALS

SUMMARY OF OBEDIENCE RECORD

TITLE	REGISTRY (AKC,CKC,UKC,STATES)	DATE	JUDGE	SCORE	COMMENTS
C.D. Leg 1					
Leg 2					
Leg 3					
C.DX. Leg 1					
Leg 2					
Leg 3					
U.D. Leg 1					
Leg 2					
Leg 3					
U.DX. Leg 1					
Leg 2					
Leg 3					
Leg 4					
Leg 5					
Leg 6					
Leg 7					
Leg 8					
Leg 9					
Leg 10					
Other – Leg 1					
Leg 2					
Leg 3					
TRACKING CERTIFIED					
TD					
TDX					

SUMMARY OF TOURNAMENTS

DATE	TOURNAMENT NAME	LOCATION	SCORE	AWARDS

WARMING UP A DOG

The purpose of a warmup is to put the dog in the best frame of mind possible to perform obedience accurately and with enthusiasm. Ideally the dog will be alert and relaxed. The warmup only deals with skills the dog already knows. You should not attempt to teach a dog something new in a warmup. The warmup is a process of evaluation, motivation, confidence building and fine tuning. It should consist of a series of "up", intense, polish exercises followed by immediate release, praise and play. Whether you are warming up for a ring or warming up for a practice session, the first 10 minutes or so that you spend training should be devoted to getting you and the dog in rhythm with each other and geared towards working as a team. Corrections in the warmup should be minimal. Praise and help are what encourage a dog to work with you.

Every warmup should be tailored to the specific dog you are training and to the mood of the dog on that day. If a dog has had a few days off from obedience work he is likely to be a little higher in energy and potentially less accurate. This dog may require a longer warmup than a dog who was just worked the night before. Too much warmup defeats the purpose. A dog who is overly warmed up will give a performance lacking luster and energy. If you feel your dog's energy or drive sinking during a warmup, stop training and put the dog back in a crate for 15 minutes. The next time to take him out to work plan to be very brief.

What exactly should you do in a warmup?

WARMUP... (cont.)

EVALUATE

Heel your dog once around in a big circle and determine how much energy, attention and rhythm the dog and you have.

↓

If the dog is very "high", or if you have no rhythm, continue in big circles in both directions until the dog settles down. You're better off to wear the dog down than to correct for enthusiasm. Keep a taut leash.

↓

Having established rhythm, attention and some energy (different for each dog) review transitions for change of pace.

↓

Review timing and footwork with the dog on about turns, right turns and left turns

↓

Practice halts in sequence and following turns to make sure you and the dog are in rhythm on the halts.

↓

Realign fronts and finishes by pointing out where the dog should be looking.

If your dog has rhythm and attention but low energy, release him and play by wrestling or tug of war with the leash.

If attention is weak, do some stationary attention exercises. Then demand more attention while moving. Be brief and enthusiastic.

If you are showing in Utility you might want to review signals or do some glove and article pivots.

If you're showing in Open, you might want to do a comefore drop on leash. To practice the turn coming off the broad jump: with the dog sitting in heel position, tell the dog stay and step to the right and back 2 steps. Now call the dog to come. This simulates the turn off the broad jump.

If you are showing in Novice, you might want to practice heeling a figure a 8 or merely a circle right to remind the dog to bend and lean into the right.

92

WARMUP....cont.

When heeling in a ring you will be in Show Mode, either on or off leash. To warm your dog up into Show Mode follow the steps below:

___ 1. Heel on a taut leash in a   Training Mode.

___ 2. Heel on a taut leash in a   Show Mode

___ 3. Heel on a loose leash in   Training Mode.

___ 4. Heel on a loose leash in   Show Mode

___ 5. Heel off leash in   Training Mode.

___ 6. Heel off leash in   Show Mode

WARMUP.... (cont.)

Always work on your dog's chronic problems in a warmup. For example, if your dog tends to forge, you will want to warmup with lots of circles to the left, left "U's", left turns, slows, and heeling backwards. If your dog tends to lag you will want to warmup with circles to the right, right turns, fasts, about turns and brisk starts.

The AKC does not permit a comprehensive warmup on show grounds. Any "drilling" of an exercise is prohibited. The dog is never to be off a leash at a show except when required in a ring. The AKC will allow limited on leash heeling and a front and finish on leash, designed to occur 5 minutes before you go into a ring.

If you need more of a warmup with your dog (and you will!) you will need to find a secluded place or go off the show grounds to accomplish this. Ideally a warmup should take 5 – 10 minutes. With some dogs in a show situation, warm them up more than once before showing with a goal of gradually bringing them up to a peak performance. A brief evaluation when you first get settled at a show will let you know where your dog's head is on any given day. Some dogs are moodier and stress more easily from travel. The distraction level of intact male dogs varies with different environments. At a large all-breed and obedience shows with dirty mats or smelly grass and crowded conditions, you are more likely to spend time working on attention then if you were showing on concrete at a quiet all-obedience event.

TRUE or FALSE
Test Your Knowledge of the AKC Rules!

In the Novice Ring:

____ 1) A six foot leash is required for the heel on leash.
____ 2) Giving a second "heel" command during heeling is permitted.
____ 3) During the stand for exam you may not pose a dog as in the breed ring.
____ 4) To begin the figure 8, you must go to the left first.
____ 5) During the heeling pattern, a judge may call a "Fast", "Halt"
____ 6) Before you tell your dog to "Stay", your hands must be off the dog.
____ 7) When you call your dog on the recall, your hands must hang naturally at your sides.
____ 8) During the heel off-leash, if both arms are at your side, only the right arm must "swing naturally."
____ 9) If your dog automatically finishes, you should always give your heel command anyway, after the judge says, "Finish".
____ 10) You may gently guide the dog between exercises by putting a finger through the collar.

In the Open Ring:

____ 1) After sending your dog on the retrieve on flat, you may adjust the position of your feet.
____ 2) You can place the dumbbell in the dog's mouth before the retrieve, but only before the judge has said, "Are your ready?"
____ 3) If you stand even with the last board during the broad jump, you will be penalized if, after you pivot, your toes are past the last board.
____ 4) A held drop signal will always result in a Non-Qualified (NQ).
____ 5) You must start your dog eight (8) feet from the broad jump, no more, no less.
____ 6) During the measurement of the dog, you must have your hands off the dog.
____ 7) A hand signal is legal for the broad jump command.
____ 8) If you require more than one re-throw, you will be penalized two (2) points for each one.
____ 9) If your dog takes the high jump on the way out to the dumbbell during the retrieve on flat, you will lose points, but not be scored zero (0).
____ 10) You may show the dog the dumbbell, before throwing it.

Rules....cont.

In the Utility Ring:

_____ 1) You may give a signal or a verbal, but not both for the go-out.

_____ 2) It is legal to put one knee on the ground when giving a glove signal to a small dog.

_____ 3) After giving the scent cue with your right hand, you may pivot and swing your arm back to your side at the same time.

_____ 4) If your dog takes a jump on the way out to go out, you will always be disqualified.

_____ 5) A handler will receive a deduction if he or she watches the placement of the gloves.

_____ 6) During the moving stand, a dog will receive a zero (0) if he sits front instead of going to heel.

_____ 7) You may give a signal and verbal command to send your dog to the article pile.

_____ 8) During the heel portion of the moving stand you can receive a score of zero (0) if the dog heels poorly (as defined by the rules governing heeling in Novice.)

_____ 9) If during the heeling portion of the signal exercise, you give a second "heel" command (signal or verbal), you will receive a zero (0).

_____ 10) Bending your knee while giving a go-out signal is permitted.

_____ 11) The moving stand exam may include the examination of the dog's mouth.

_____ 12) On the directed retrieve, if you under pivot or over pivot to a glove you may be scored a zero (0).

_____ 13) If, on the Go-Out the dog reaches the gate before he is told to turn and sit you may receive a substantial deduction.

WHAT'S WRONG WITH THIS PICTURE?

Below is a scene from a dog show. Study it carefully.

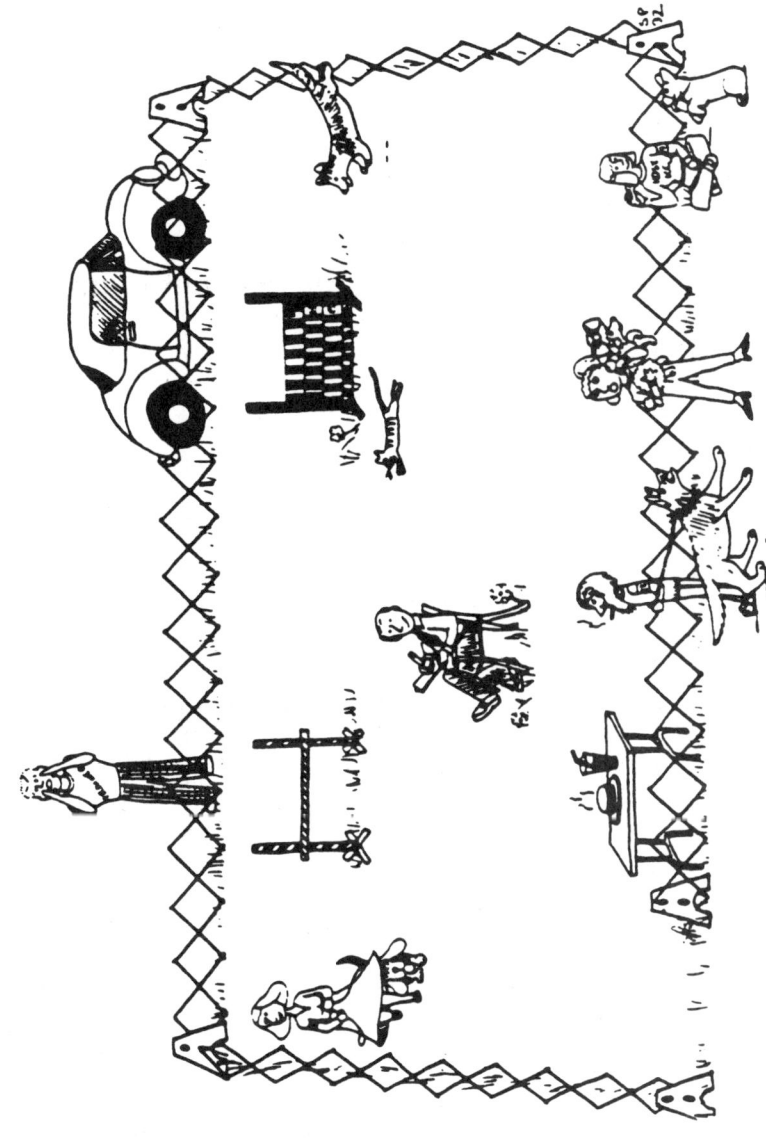

What's wrong...Cont'.

A) How many things can you find that are against AKC regulations:

1) _____
2) _____
3) _____
4) _____
5) _____
6) _____
7) _____
8) _____

B) How many things can you find that are working against your dog's performance but are not against the AKC regulations:

1) _____
2) _____
3) _____
4) _____
5) _____
6) _____
7) _____
8) _____

(Check the back of this Workbook, for the correct responses)

ANCHORING

So much of your dog's performance in a ring depends on his/her state of mind at the time the dog is in the ring. Throughout your dog's training you work to set up situations where the dog will respond correctly to a command regardless of the state of mind he is in at the time. The reality of the situation is that certain states of mind are easier to elicit a response from.

For example:
> A male dog, just having sniffed a bitch in heat smell in the grass is going to have a completely different response to a "find it" command then if there was no bitch in heat smell.

A sound sensitive dog will have a different response to a command immediately following a strong wind which rattles gates and makes tents flap.

If a smell or a sound can change a dog's state of mind in an instant, is there a way to cause a positive state of mind change just as quickly?

Have you ever been driving in your car when a song came on the radio, which all of a sudden made you feel happy?

Maybe the song was an "Oldie" and reminded you of a time in your past when you were first in love. Your state of mind has been instantly changed in a positive way because your brain has anchored a feeling to a sound.

Do dogs anchor feelings to sounds as well?

           Y E S   **N O**

What happens to your dog's behavior and attitude if you rattle a box of dog biscuits?

_____

_____

...take out a tennis ball...?

_____

_____

...pick up your car keys....?

_____

_____

While it is not possible to take cookies, keys or tennis balls into a ring with you, you can take words! Let's suppose you had a word that was anchored into positive feelings and attentiveness for your dog. This could come in very useful in a ring situation!

ANCHORING... Cont.

HOW TO ANCHOR A WORD:

1) Pick a nonsense word that only you will know and use.
2) Find a time in your dog's life when he is really excited and happy about something. Maybe it's when you feed him treats, or play Frisbee, or let him run laps in the back yard. Whatever it is, it's a very positive state of mind.
3) For three (3) weeks, every time this activity is about to occur and <u>during</u> the activity, repeat your nonsense word.
4) You should start to see the dog begin to associate the activity with the word and anticipate the positive state of mind.

Note: You will need to continually reinforce the anchor word, but you can do this at times other than at shows. (It's like recharging a battery!)

WHEN TO USE THE ANCHOR WORD:

Don't abuse the ability to change your dogs state of mind in an instant. Save it for when you really need it. If you were to use it every time you entered a ring you would soon wear it out. Suppose you heard the song that made you feel happy, every other day..... Would you still have the same reaction?

Use your anchor word when something unexpected happens in a ring and you feel like you have lost your dog for the moment.

Use your anchor word on the way to an exercise or just before your walk into the ring.

Your anchor word should be very unique and you should say it in a special, excited way. Always keep it reinforced and ready to use.

Some dogs anchor easier than others and some can be anchored best into a touch rather than a sound. Think about how you would anchor your dog's positive state to a certain way you pet him or scratch him.

HIERARCHY

Below is a list of things that are important to us in life.

Order this list according to what you value most:

A Leg on a Degree	1 _____
Adventure	2 _____
Attentive Heeling	3 _____
Comfort	4 _____
Family	5 _____
Health	6 _____
Love	7 _____
Security	8 _____
Straight Sits	9 _____
Wealth	10 _____

Sometimes it pays to put things in perspective !

J U M P I N G   J U M B L E

Regarding Jumping ....

Use a **RENTFIFED** verbal command for each jump, in direct jumping.

___ ___ ___ ___ ___ ___ ___ ___

On retrieve over the high jump, teach the **TRERUN** before you ever throw a dumbbell over the jump.

___ ___ ___ ___ ___ ___

When giving a directed jumping signal, show the dog your **LAMP** before lifting the hand signal.

___ ___ ___ ___

If the dog takes the **GROWN** jump, continue to hold the signal, until the dog knows he's made a mistake, then walk back and start again.

___ ___ ___ ___ ___

102

Jumble...Cont'.

The Utility ring is diamond shaped, so when giving the signal, position your arm _ _ _ _ _ _ of your body.

103

"TO PINCH OR ....
...... NOT TO PINCH ??"
THAT IS THE QUESTION !!

Read the following retrieve scenarios. After reading through them, decide whether you would pinch (P) or help (H). Then read the explanations and decide which Help (H) or Pinch (P) explanation best explains your reasons.

SCENE ONE:

Heidi takes her great Dane Shelby to an obedience club for work on retrieve. The dog has had some proofing prior to this session. Heidi arrives, goes into a ring and throws the dumbbell. On the first throw, the dumbbell lands about three feet from a poodle doing a down stay. The poodle remains in a down, and although Shelby approaches the dumbbell with some hesitation, she picks it up and trots back to Heidi. She is praised profusely and Heidi sets up to throw again. This time the dumbbell lands in the same spot, only this time when Shelby approaches the dumbbell, the poodle bares her teeth and growls. Shelby tucks her tail and heads back to Heidi. What should Heidi do?

- A. Pinch: Shelby already showed that she could retrieve in this situation s few moments prior to this. She obviously feels feels that she has a choice and should be corrected.
- B. Help: A great Dane that retrieves anything should be helped, never corrected. Danes have extremely sensitive ears and pinching can result in loss of enthusiasm.
- C. Pinch: The poodle is a lot smaller than Shelby. If the situation had been another Dane or large dog growling at her, then help would be appropriate. In this case, she was just being a sissy.
- D. Help: Although it is true that she retrieved only moments before, the situation had drastically changed. Shelby was afraid that the poodle might act on it's threat (growling) and so she went back to Heidi in a state of fear. Heidi should help her to the dumbbell, and show her it is truly OK to retrieve in this situation (all the while keeping her eye on the poodle.)

Answer: _____

Pinch...Cont.

SCENE TWO:

Susan and her golden Maggie have been working on her fully proofed retrieve for about six (6) months. The dog is doing very well and this is not and never has been a problem area for her. She takes the dog to a covered area during a rainstorm to do an Open run through. The dog is doing a lovely job, confident and happy, although the noise from the rain could clearly be a distraction. Susan sets up to do a retrieve on flat, throws the dumbbell, and watches it land about six (6) inches past the covered area (aka in the rain!). She sends Maggie and the dog runs out, puts one foot out in the rain, clearly intending to get the dumbbell, and at that moment a loud clap of thunder booms. Maggie wheels around and races back to Susan. Susan slowly walks with Maggie out to the dumbbell (in the rain) pointing to it and says "Take It". Maggie, not totally confident picks up quickly and brings it to her. The next time, Susan sets them up two feet from the edge of the covering, as she wants Maggie to sense her closeness as she works out her fear during this retrieve. Time and time again, Maggie either starts out and runs back to Susan without the dumbbell, or totally refuses to go out at all. Her body posturing during all of this is tail tucked, ears back and she holds her head ducked, avoiding eye contact with Susan. Susan's reaction was one of patience, she would either walk out to the dumbbell, pointing, and then Maggie would retrieve it. She even backed up and had the dumbbell not out in the rain – at that point Maggie would pick it up. After 10 or 15 times of this, what should she do?

Pinch ???....cont'.

A. **Help:** This dog is obviously afraid, and should not be pinched. Besides, the dog was retrieving well prior to this and she is, after all, a golden, so she should continue in the help pattern she is in.

B. **Pinch:** Sometimes a dog clings to fear and can't be helped out of it. At this point, Susan needs to let Maggie know that whatever she is afraid of out in the rain is not half as bad as what will happen to her (a pinch) if she does not retrieve. A dog needs to trust that you will never let anything bad happen to it, and sometimes the dog's fear is so intense that it needs to be helped by being corrected.

C. **Help:** Why should a dog be made to retrieve in the rain? Chances are, if it is raining at a show, she will pull the dog from competition. And, if it starts to rain at a show during the retrieve on flat, then she should just accept her bad luck and not worry about it. How often is that going to happen anyway?

D. **Pinch:** The dog is not really afraid. Maybe she was after the first boom of thunder, but after she had been helped a number of times and there was no thunder anymore, the dog knew nothing was going to hurt her. This is a classic case of a dog thinking, "hey, if I pretend I'm afraid, mom doesn't put pressure on me, and even makes my job easier by moving it out of the rain." After the first time (or maximum the second time) she was helped, the dog should have been pinched.

Answer: _____

Pinch ???....Cont'.

SCENE THREE:

Joyce has a three year old Brussels Griffon named Sam. Sam is no stranger to a proofed retrieve. He has been trained with proofing from the very beginning Sam has two U.D. legs and is a very seasoned dog. One day Joyce takes Sam out in their backyard for a quick glove session. She expects nothing out of the ordinary (a mistake!), as this happens to be Sam's favorite exercise. Sam, seeing the gloves in her hand begins a happy little dance, knowing what is next. Joyce has a friend set out the gloves and her friend tells her "Glove 3". Joyce gives Sam the command to "heel" and they execute a perfect pivot. Joyce leans over, gives a clear signal and tells Sam to "Take it". Sam races out reaches down to pick up the glove and stops. He looks at Joyce and to retrieve glove #2. Joyce stops him verbally and sets up to do this again. Before she sends him, she goes out and looks at where glove #3 is sitting. What she notices is that the grass is noticeably higher around this glove than any of the others and that the morning dew has made the long grass very wet. She goes back to Sam, pivots and sends him again. This time as, he is half way to number 3, he takes a hard left and confidently goes to #2 again. Joyce again stops Sam verbally and sets up to do it again. What should Joyce do?

Pinch??....cont'.

A. **Help:** Brussels have pushed in faces and often have a hard time breathing. Expecting him to stick his face in a pile of long wet grass is a little much. She should help him by either moving the gloves to a shorter, dryer area of grass, or move to a concrete or matted area.

B. **Pinch:** The first time he went to the correct glove but then ran to the other he should have been pinched. Any dog who has two legs on a U.D. and is no stranger to a proofed retrieve should be corrected. Typically, little dogs tend to try and manipulate their handlers using their size (or lack of) as if to say "this is too hard for poor little me". This dog should have been corrected on the first time.

C. **Help:** She should continue sending and stopping him until he understands that he cannot go to another glove just because he like the grass conditions better. Eventually, a seasoned and willing dog like this will go to the correct glove because he sees that it displeases his owner when he goes to the other. A correction to a happy, willing dog like this will only hurt his feelings and possibly confuse him. After all, he only needs one more leg — why risk creating problems with the exercise?

D. **Pinch:** Joyce was correct in not pinching Sam the first time he retrieved. She was also right in checking out the area from his point of view to make sure there was not anything out there that may have hurt or frightened him. However, after she knew the circumstances of his refusal (looking for the glove in a shorter, dryer area), she should pinch him. Her correction would say to him "You must retrieve this glove in this situation. There is nothing here that will injure you."

Answer: _____

Pinch??? ....Cont'.

SCENE FOUR:

Kathie has a Bichon named Misha. He has had his U.D. for about a year. Lately Misha has had a confidence problem with his articles. He happily runs out to the pile and sniffs the articles. When he finds the one with her scent on it he picks it up, and wagging his tail trots one or two steps into her drops it, goes back to the pike, rechecks, and then eventually goes back to the article he correctly picked up first, and trots briskly in. Misha does this on both articles, metal and leather, each and every time. He is always up and willing to start articles, and never shows signs of being stressed. This has gone on for approximately one month. What should Kathie do?

A. Help: The dog is working out a confidence problem. Eventually he will realize that he is always correct on his first try, and he will stop dropping the article. Time will help this problem.

B. Pinch: The length of time that this problem has gone on is the key in deciding what to do. The dog has now gotten into a comfortable pattern of picking up, dropping and re-checking the pile. There is no visible stress signs on him, so we must now teach him that the first one he picks up is the one he must bring in. When he drops the article Kathie should walk in slowly, isolate the article he dropped, and pinch as she points to it. She should then praise profusely.

C. Help: The handler should go back to basic retrieving with a dumbbell. The dog seems to need proofing on the "hold" and "return" part of the retrieve exercise. When articles are re-started there should only be two articles in the pile (including the scented one) for about six (6) weeks.

D. Pinch: This dog should be pinched because he is distracted. He goes back to the pile as an excuse to buy more time to avoid going back to the handler. He obviously dislikes the exercise and wants to avoid having to do another article. Bichons often seem to be happy, because the breed does not show stress. They always trot briskly and wag their tails. This is in the breed standard and often fools new owners.

OBEDIENCE CROSSWORD PUZZLE

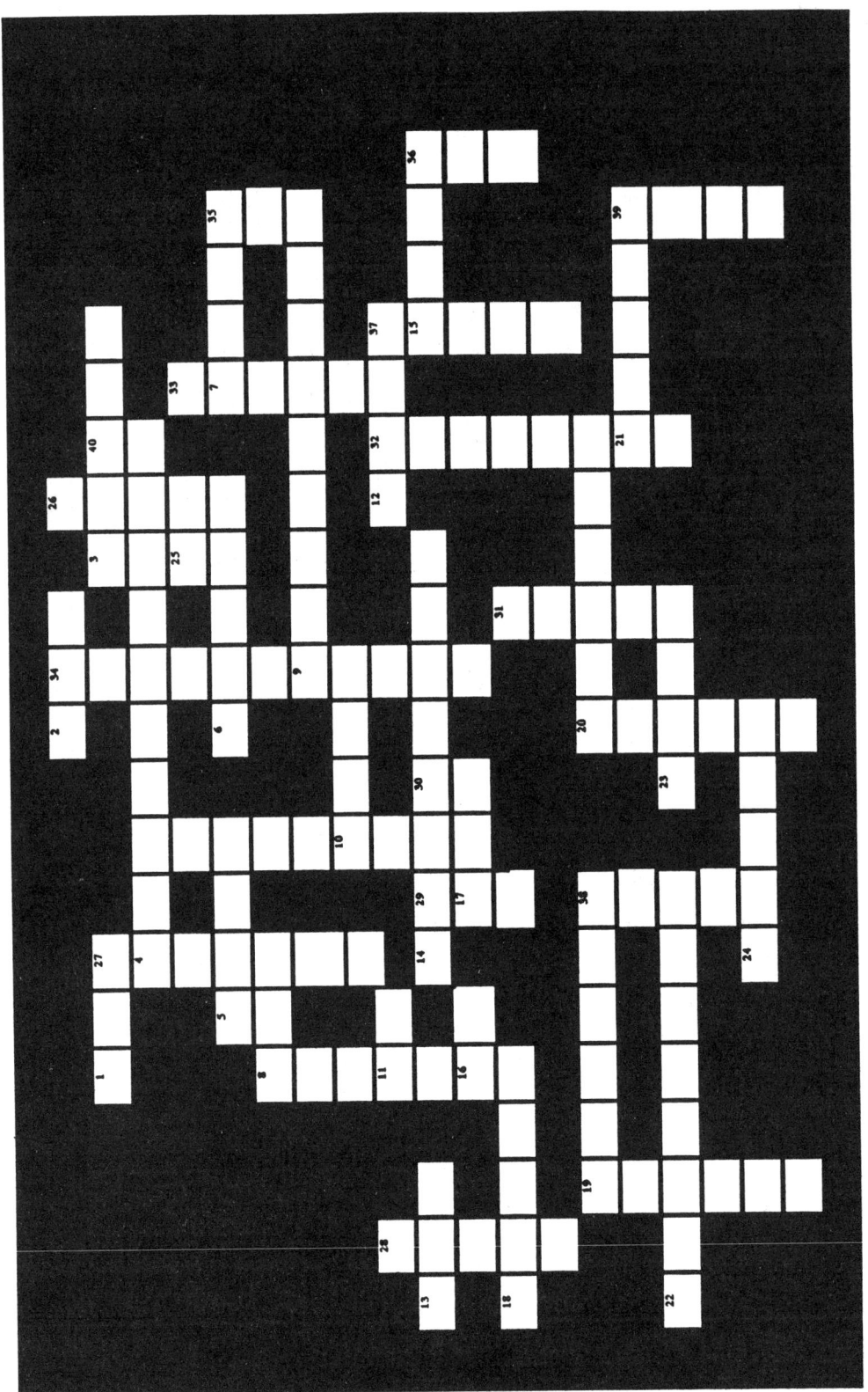

OBEDIENCE CROSSWORD PUZZLE

ACROSS

1. The dog learns to retrieve because of a correction given to his _____ which leaves his neck and mouth free to pick up the dumbbell.
2. To show your dog at a match without competing.
3. _____ Tests the dog's understanding of an exercise.
4. When you show, you are asking for one judge's _____ one, two.
6. When using a hand signal and voice commands as in directed jumping or gloves the hand and voice must be properly _____.
7. Heel position is the dog's _____ and shoulders, in line with your left hip.
8. Open title.
9. Enthusiasm, style and flash
10. Found at dog shows to provide shade.
11. Tracking Title
12. Ground poles are used to teach a dog to _____.
13. Judges want dogs who exhibit _____ and willingness.
14. Putting your feet in the right places to cue the dog on heeling.
15. Highest Obedience degree.
16. Champion.
17. One
18. Turning in place.
19. Corrections are given when a dog feels he has a _____.
20. In the drop on recall, the down command will _____ the come command.
21. Used to guide and teach a dog.
22. Permitting
23. When a dog is first learning it is important not t _____ him.
24. Judges take off points for handlers who _____ their dogs into sits on the halt.
25. Distracting noise at a dog show.

DOWN

3. Portable jumps are now being made from PVC _____.
5. _____ Herding Title.
8. While heeling the dog should not make _____ with your left leg.
19. When the leash comes off in the off-leash heeling, the dog heels because of what you can do to him not because of the _____ he is wearing.
20. Used to teach a straight sit front and a straight "Go-out".
26. A jump where length is more important than height.
27. A good handler appears calm and _____.
28. Leash used for short-legged dogs.
29. Go
30. In direction of.
31. The prong collar is used to _____ the dog's neck with even distribution of pressure.
32. Used to shade judges at outdoor shows.
33. Used to keep heeling smooth.
34. Moving stand for _____.
35. A dog is a _____ animal which is why he likes a crate.
36. Heel position puts the dog in line with your left _____.
37. To teach a dog where to focus his eyes for front or heel, _____ with your finger.
38. Minimum distance dumbbell must land on the other side of the high jump is _____ feet.
39. Take it, _____ and Give are three commands often used sequentially, but never repeated.
40. "Sit" is the _____ Switch of attention.

TASK PROJECT CHARTS

In the pages that follow you will find every obedience exercise broken down into the steps necessary to completely teach the exercise according to <u>Beyond Basic Dog Training.</u> All too often, handlers skip steps in training. This creates a weak link in the dog's understanding of an exercise. Weak links tend to break after time and you will usually find yourself having to back up and teach the steps you originally left out.

When the dog demonstrates that he/she can complete the task described, you may immediately move on to the next step in sequential order. Some dogs will complete numerous steps in one training session. You may find a step that is difficult for you or your dog, where you will spend a few training sessions trying to complete a single step. All dogs learn at different rates and different dogs learn certain exercises faster then others. By completing the boxes to the right of the tasks you will always know at a glance which step of an exercise you are working on.

It is important to read the task descriptions carefully. Some steps ask for the dog to be able to DO something. This is very different from a step that asks for a dog to show <u>confidence</u> doing something.

If you are not sure whether your dog has fully completed the task and is ready to go on, ask an instructor or training friend to help you "read" the dog.

To review how to teach the various tasks, refer to:
> **<u>Beyond Basic Dog Training</u>** (Howell – Revised Edition)

H E E L I N G

STEPS: COMPLETED   DATE   COMMENTS

1. The handler knows and can execute correct footwork necessary to do a start, halt, right turn, left turn, about turn, transitions to and from slow and fast.   ☐   _____   ☐

2. On an attention command the dog will sit and look up at the handler.   ☐   _____   ☐

3. The dog can do stationary attention (sitting and looking up with proofing.)   ☐   _____   ☐

4. The dog will allow the handler to cradle his head up and will stand up from a sit without dropping his head.   ☐   _____   ☐

5. The dog can walk 2 steps with the handler holding his head (the handler's left hand cradles the dog's chin.) The dog doesn't fight his head being held.   ☐   _____   ☐

6. The dog can walk 10 steps with his head held up. (The lead is taut to keep the dog in the correct position.)   ☐   _____   ☐

7. The dog will trot with his head being held up in a big circle to the left and then to the right.   ☐   _____   ☐

8. The dog can walk 10 steps with his head up without the handler holding the head. The hand in under the chin only for the first 1–2 steps. If the head drops, the handler gives a correction and the heads will come back up.   ☐   _____   ☐

9. The dog can do step #8 without the handler holding his head.   ☐   _____   ☐

10. The dog understands that the moving focal point is a spot 1–2 inches above the dog's eye on the left side of the handler's body.   ☐   _____   ☐

Heeling.... Cont.

STEPS: COMPLETED DATE COMMENTS

11. The dog can change pace, "normal–slow–normal–fast–normal", with his head up, watching the focal point. ☐

12. The dog can heel with attention in a straight line at different speeds with light to heavy proofing:
    a. Someone is playing Judge and walking near the dog and handler.
    b. Someone is talking to the dog.
    c. Someone is offering food to the dog while he is heeling. (The lead is still taut.) ☐

13. The dog can do "halts, about turns, right turns and left turns" correctly with attention and the handler helping. The left hand cradles the chin when necessary. ☐

14. The dog can do step #10 without the handler helping with the left hand. If the head drops, the handler can correct and get the attention back. (The lead is still taut.) ☐

15. The dog can do "halts" and "turns" with light to heavy proofing, (same proofing as used for step #12) with a taut lead. ☐

16. The dog can do step #12 on a loose leash. ☐

17. The dog can heel with attention with the leash tied around the handler's waist. If the dog gets out of heel position he will move back into position when the handler reaches for his head. (Off leash corrections.) ☐

18. The dog can heel with attention (step #17) with proofing. ☐

19. The dog can heel with attention off lead with confidence and accuracy. ☐

20. The dog can do step #19 with proofing. ☐

F I G U R E 8

STEPS: COMPLETED   DATE   COMMENTS

1. The handler understands what an obedience "figure 8" looks like and can walk it correctly without a dog. ☐ _____ ☐

2. The dog knows how to spiral right and left. ☐ _____ ☐

3. The dog knows to go slowly around the post to his left and go fast around the post to his right, with attention. The handler uses cue words and exaggerates going slowly and going fast. The dog is on a taut lead. ☐ _____ ☐

4. The dog can do step #3 when the handler maintains constant speed and still uses cue words. ☐ _____ ☐

5. The dog can use his rear properly in order to maintain correct heel position with the use of a dowel. The dog is still on a taut leash. ☐ _____ ☐

6. The dog can do step #5 on a loose leash. ☐ _____ ☐

7. The dog can do the figure 8 correctly on a taut leash with light proofing: posts talking to the dog, "Judge" talking to the dog. ☐ _____ ☐

8. The dog can do step #7 with moderate proofing: around 3 posts, abouts and U-turns in the figure 8, halts on the outside of the posts. ☐ _____ ☐

9. The dog can do step #7 with heavy proofing: posts offering the dog food, posts dressed funny. ☐ _____ ☐

10. The dog can do Novice ring procedure figure 8 with light, moderate and heavy proofing. ☐ _____ ☐

11. The dog can do correct figure 8 with the leash tied around the handler's waist with light, moderate and heavy proofing. ☐ _____ ☐

12. The dog can do Open ring procedure figure 8 with all levels of proofing. ☐ _____ ☐

THE RECALL

COMPLETED   DATE   COMMENTS

STEPS:

1. The dog can be gently coiled in on a loose lead to the handler on the "come" command. The dog is no more than 6' away. The dog doesn't need to sit front but must physically touch the handler. The handler should verbally praise as long as the dog is looking at him. Only give one "Come" command.

2. The dog will do step #1 without being coiled into the handler. The dog has learned that "Boogie Dog" strikes for no response to "Come".

3. The dog will do step #2 with heavy distractions: food, animals, open house doors, open car doors.

4. The dog will do a "Karate Chop" recall with confidence (only for dogs who can do a reliable sit stay). See page 120 of Beyond Basic Dog Training.

5. The dog will do a recall (from release or sit stay) on a long line with light to heavy distractions: different locations, someone talking to the dog, offering food or petting, other dogs playing. No sit front is required.

6. The dog will do off lead recall and will sit front (note necessarily straight.) The handler begins 6' away and works to full distance. Praise as the dog comes in.

7. The dog will do step #6 with the proofing done in step 5.

8. The dog will do Ring Procedure Recall and will think about a straight sit front. The dog knows how to move his body to accomplish a straight sit.

DOWN EXERCISE (for STAYS)

(Choose the method of downing a dog that will best suit your dog, regardless of his age.)

| | COMPLETED | DATE | COMMENTS |

STEPS: (for an adult dog with sound temperament)

1. The dog will down on command and signal without the handler needing to give a correction or pressure on the dog's withers. The dog is lying on his left hip, and the handler is in the heel position, but bent over. See "Adult Down" page 105 in <u>Beyond Basic Dog Training</u>

2. The dog will do step 1 and remain in the Down for 10 seconds while the handler stands up in heel position. The dog gets up on "Okay!"

STEPS: (for short legged dogs.)

1. The dog will go into a Down when the handler slides the front feet forward with the right hand and puts pressure on the dogs withers with the left hand. The dog is sitting in heel position and the owner is crouched down.

2. The dog will do step 1 with only verbal command and signal and remain in the Down for 10 seconds until he is given and "Okay!" release.

Down..Cont'.

STEPS: (for puppies)   COMPLETED   DATE   COMMENTS

1. The puppy is in a sit in heel position. The puppy will allow the handler to gently slide the front legs forward into a down. The handler is on his knees or bent down. The handler's left arm across the puppy's shoulders prevents him from getting up. The puppy is lying on his left hip. ☐ _____ ☐

2. The puppy will go into a down from a sit in heel position without help from the handler. ☐ _____ ☐

3. The puppy will do step 2 and remain in down for 10 seconds until the "Okay!" release. ☐ _____ ☐

STEPS: (Foot drop for large or resistant dogs.)

1. The dog will down on command when the handler steps into the leash with the left foot and gives upward pressure with the lead held in the right hand. See page 109 in _Beyond Basic Dog Training_ ☐ _____ ☐

2. The dog will so step 1 and remain in the Down for 10 seconds while the handler keeps his left foot on the lead to prevent the dog from getting up. ☐ _____ ☐

3. The dog will down on verbal command and signal only and remain in heel position for 10 seconds until given an "Okay!" release. The dog is lying on his left hip. ☐ _____ ☐

DOWN STAY

STEPS:	COMPLETED	DATE	COMMENTS

1. The dog will do Down Stay on a 6' lead with the handler in heel position for 30 seconds. Stay signal is the same as the sit stay signal. ☐

2. The dog will do step (1) one in three (3) different locations (Light proofing). ☐

3. The dog will down and stay for 30 seconds with the handler 2' in front of the dog. The handler moves enthusiastically to encourage the dog to get up. The dog still on lead (moderate proofing) ☐

4. The dog will do step 3 while the handler gives steady gently pressure on the lead. Pressure on lead teaches the dog to remain on the left hip and keep the left foot tucked. (moderate proofing) ☐

5. The dog will hold the stay with heavy proofing: the other person talking to the dog, petting him, or offering him food if he comes to them, and with other dogs on the Down Stay. ☐

6. The dog will do a 1 minute Down Stay on a long line. The handler gradually increases distance to 15'. ☐

7. The dog will hold the Down Stay for light to heavy proofing with the handler at the end of the 15' long line. ☐

8. The dog will do a Down Stay off lead with the handler 6' away, with light to heavy proofing. ☐

9. The dog will do step 8 with the handler 15 away with light to heavy proofing. ☐

10. The dog will do ring procedure down stay (with a group of dogs.) ☐

SIT STAY

STEPS:	COMPLETED	DATE	COMMENTS

1. On leash, the dog will hold Sit Stay for five (5) counts with the handler directly in front of the dog (toe to toe.) The handler pivots on the right foot to get in front and returns to heel position. The same path, the handler gives the stay signal with the left hand (palm in front of the dog's nose) and has the dog hold the position while being verbally praised for five (5) counts before releasing. The dog is helped (repositioned silently) if he makes a mistake, followed by praise. ☐

2. The dog will do step # (1) with the handler GRADUALLY increasing distance from the dog to 6 feet and increasing time to one (1) minute. ☐

3. The dog will hold the Sit Stay when the handler returns to heel position by going around behind the dog. The handler keeps the leash on the right side of the dog and touches the dog's head the first few times to aid the dog in holding the stay when the handler leaves the dog's eyesight. ☐

4. The dog will hold the sit stay up to one (1) minute while the handler tempts the dog to break by moving right, left, jumping up and down, turning around, sitting on the ground, singing out loud, etc. The dog is still on the 6 feet leash and helped (repositioned) if he is tempted to move. ☐

5. The dog will hold the Sit Stay on the 6' leash for one (1) minute while another person lightly distracts someone: walking around the dog, another dog playing, different locations. ☐

Sit Stay...Cont'.

STEPS: COMPLETED   DATE   COMMENTS

6. The dog will do step # 5 with moderate distractions: other person calling the dog ("puppy come"), other person asking the dog to down or giving an "Okay" release.   ☐   _____   ☐

7. The dog will do step # 5 with heavy distractions: other person offering food to the dog, other person throwing balls or toys in front of him, trained dogs being called off of the stays beside him.   ☐   _____   ☐

8. The dog will do steps # 5, # 6 and # 7 off leash.   ☐   _____   ☐

9. The dog will hold the Sit Stay with the handler 10' away with same type of proofs as in steps 5, 6 and 7. Time gradually increased to two (2) minutes.   ☐   _____   ☐

10. The dog will do step # 9 with the handler 20' away.   ☐   _____   ☐

11. The dog will do step # 10 for three (3) minutes.   ☐   _____   ☐

12. The dog will do step # 11 thirty (30) feet away.   ☐   _____   ☐

13. The dog will do ring procedures (Novice) sit stay.   ☐   _____   ☐

Stand For Examination

	COMPLETED	DATE	COMMENTS
STEPS:			
1. The dog will stand on command and signal, with his head up with the help of the handler's left foot or hand.	☐	_____	☐
2. The dog will stand on command and signal, with his head up without help.	☐	_____	☐
3. The dog will hold the stand while handler gently presses on his back with the palm of the left hand.	☐	_____	☐
4. The dog will hold the stand when the handler stands up into the heel position.	☐	_____	☐
5. The dog will do a Stand Stay on lead with the handler directly in front of him for 30 seconds.	☐	_____	☐
6. The dog will do a Stand Stay with the handler 6' in front applying steady pressure on the lead. The dog resists pressure and doesn't move.	☐	_____	☐
7. The dog will hold a Sit Stay in heel position while being touched and talked to by a friendly stranger.	☐	_____	☐

Stand..... Cont'.

STEPS: COMPLETED   DATE   COMMENTS

8. The will hold a Sit Stay on lead while being touched by the friendly stranger with the handler 6' in front.   ☐   _____   ☐

9. The dog will do step #7 off lead   ☐   _____   ☐

10. The dog will hold a Stand Stay off lead in heel position while being touched by a stranger.   ☐   _____   ☐

11. The dog will do a Stand Stay off lead while being touched by a stranger with the handler 6' in front.   ☐   _____   ☐

12. The dog will do step #10 while a stranger examines the dog from head to toe,   ☐   _____   ☐

13. The dog will do a ring procedure Stand Stay with light to heavy proofing:
   a) The dog will do a Stand Stay with confidence in three (3) different environments.
   b) With different types of people playing "Judge": (wearing a hat, gloved, etc.)
   c) With different approaches of people playing "Judge": (staggering, hesitant, briskly, roughly.)
   ☐   _____   ☐

FINISH

	COMPLETED	DATE	COMMENTS

STEPS:

1. The dog will let the handler guide him around with his head held or baited up to heel position on lead. Handler steps back on the right foot after giving the heel command and moves the right foot back up to meet the left as the dog comes around to heel position. The handler points to heel position with the right hand as the dog comes around. The handler commands "Sit" just before the dog reaches heel position. ☐

2. The dog will move on command to heel position with his head up on lead without the handler moving. The handler points out heel position with the right hand as the dog moves around the handler to heel position. ☐

3. The dog will finish on command off lead. The handler still points out heel position. ☐

4. The dog will do step #3 without the handler pointing out heel position. The handler may command "Sit" just before the dog reaches heel position. ☐

5. The dog will do step #3 with light proofing: ☐
   a) Someone playing "Judge".
   b) The dog will do the Finish confidently in 3 different training locations.
   c) The dog won't finish on any other word or on the dog's name.

6. The dog will do confident finishes with medium proofing: ☐
   a) Someone offering distractions as the dog goes behind the handler.
   b) Someone talking to the dog before the handler gives the finish command.

7. The dog will do a confident finish with heavy proofing: ☐
   a) Someone petting the dog as the handler give the command to finish.
   b) Someone offering food as the dog moves behind the handler.

FRONTS

STEPS: COMPLETED DATE COMMENTS

1. The dog will come on command on a 6' leash and sit front correctly (tuck sit) from a comefore or karate chop recall. The dog is looking up at the handler and resting his chin on top of the handler's hands. See pare 124 of (the new updated edition.) <u>Beyond Basic Dog Training</u>

2. The dog will do step # 1 with the handler changing direction as the dog comes to sit front. The handler moves laterally and uses his knee or leg to gently nudge the dog if he appears to be about to sit crooked.

3. The dog will come and sit front (front end straight) from 6' away off leash. The handler points out front before calling the dog, returns hands to the proper position when calling the dog, and points to front again as the dog comes.

4. The dog will walk through chutes confidently.

5. The dog will come through chutes on command and sit front in proper position with attention from just outside the chutes on leash.

6. The dog will do step # 5, 4 feet outside the chutes.

7. The dog will do step # 6 off leash.

Fronts....Cont'.

STEPS: COMPLETED   DATE   COMMENTS

8. The dog will do step # 7 when he is left sitting off center to the right and to the left of the handler. The handler still points to the focal point. See page 128 of (the new updated edition.) <u>Beyond Basic Dog Training</u> ☐ _____ ☐

9. The dog will come from 10' away and line up front and rear end correctly when foot is used as a GUIDE to replace the chutes. The dog is off leash and the handler points out front. ☐ _____ ☐

10. The dog understands how to move his rear end laterally right or left when the handler uses the knee on the dog's shoulder and uses gentle steady pressure on leash towards the handler's midline. The leash prevents the dog's head from passing midline of the handler's body. The handlers' legs are slightly apart and bent to make a chute effect. ☐ _____ ☐

11. If the dog is too short to benefit from the knee on the dog's shoulder, the handler's foot is used to gently touch the side of the rear likely to be crooked. The leash prevents the dog from passing midline of the handler. ☐ _____ ☐

12. The dog will move his rear end laterally into a correct sit front when the handler uses the knee on the correct shoulder or foot for small dogs. The dog is off leash and can do the exercise from any distance or angle away from the handler. ☐ _____ ☐

The "High" & "Bar" Jumps

STEPS: COMPLETED   DATE   COMMENTS

1. Dog on a 6' lead will jump on command "HUP" or "BAR" while walking (not heeling) with the handler. The command is given 15' in front of the jump. The jump is set at 1/3 of the dog's full jump height. ☐ _____ ☐

2. The dog will do step #1 off lead. ☐ _____ ☐

3. The dog will do an off lead recall over a low jump on the command "HUP" or "BAR". The handler shows the dog jump with a hand signal before commanding. ☐ _____ ☐

4. The dog will do steps 1, 2 & 3 with a dumbbell in his mouth (the dog is responsible at this stage in keeping the dumbbell in his mouth. The dog is already taught to retrieve off the floor. ☐ _____ ☐

5. The dog will do a recall over a low jump on command with a dumbbell in his mouth wherever the handler sits him (angle jumping). ☐ _____ ☐

6. The dog on a 6' lead will hold the Stay while the dumbbell is tossed over the jump and on command "HUP" will jump, on "TAKE IT" will pickup the dumbbell and on "HUP" will jump back over the jump and sit front without mouthing the dumbbell. Jump height is 8" or lower for small dogs. ☐ _____ ☐

7. The dog will do step #6 without the "TAKE IT" command or second "HUP". ☐ _____ ☐

8. The dog will do step #7 off lead. ☐ _____ ☐

"H" & "B" Jump... Cont'.

STEPS: COMPLETED   DATE   COMMENTS

9. The dog will retrieve, over 'High' or 'Bar' jump, the dumbbell that's thrown 15' in a straight line.   Gradually increase the height of the jump.   ☐   _____   ☐

10. The dog will do step #9 with light proofing:
    a) angle throws.,
    b) other person playing judge,
    c) other person standing near thrown dumbbell.   ☐   _____   ☐

11. The dog will do step #9 with moderate proofing:
    a) strange looking jump,
    b) other person standing near thrown dumbbell talking to the dog tempting him to forget what he's doing,
    c) dumbbell thrown in high grass.   ☐   _____   ☐

12. The dog will do step #9 with heavy proofing:
    a) High Jump – Flat Retrieve Confusion (see page 198 of Beyond Basic Dog Training),
    b) In and out jumping,
    c) tossed dumbbell under a table or chair,
    d) other person tempting dog with food as he heads for the dumbbell.   ☐   _____   ☐

The "Broad" Jump

COMPLETED   DATE   COMMENTS

STEPS:

1. The dog will confidently jump on lead with the handler with two (2) boards plus a bar set at a low height on the command, "Fido Over".

2. The dog will do step #1 off lead.

3. The dog will do an on lead Recall over the jump with the handler facing the dog across the jump. The command is "Fido, Over".

4. The dog will do Step #3 off lead. The dog and handler are approximately 10' from the Jump.

5. The dog will do a Recall over the jump with two boards (plus a bar) set full distance. Chicken wire is used only if the dog has stepped between the boards.

6. The dog will jump 2 boards full distance with the bar. The bar set up is missing one upright. Chicken wire is used only if needed.

7. The dog will Jump 2 boards full distance with no uprights. Chicken wire is used if needed again. Bar is on the ground.

8. The dog will jump 2 boards full distance without the bar. Chicken wire used if needed again.

Broad...Cont'.

STEPS: COMPLETED DATE COMMENTS

9. The dog will jump 2 boards full distance with handler's left shoulder facing dog. Handler pivots 90 degrees to the right as the dog reaches him and helps the dog sit front. No wire unless needed. ☐ _____

10. The dog will do step #9 as the handler gradually works his way to the side of the jump, around the gate. ☐ _____

11. The dog will jump 2 boards full distance with the handler in line with the jump and gate used to prevent the dog from turning to soon and cutting the jump (see diagrams on page 209 of <u>Beyond Basic Dog Training</u>). Handler pivots 90 degrees right when the dog is in mid-air. ☐ _____

12. The dog will do step #11 with the handler in correct position at the side of the jump. Handler pivots 90 degrees right when the dog is in mid-air and runs backwards pointing out front to ensure a brisk front. ☐ _____

13. The dog will do the broad jump with the required number of boards and gate. ☐ _____

14. The dog will do step #13 with the handler using his knee or foot to prevent the dog from cutting the corner of the jump. Handler can also from time to time run past the dog as he jumps to prevent a premature turn. ☐ _____

Broad Jump .... cont'

STEPS: COMPLETED DATE COMMENTS

15. The dog will do the ring procedure broad jump with light proofing: ☐ _____ [ ]
    a) The dog can do the broad jumps correctly and confidently in three different locations.
    b) With another person playing "Judge".

16. The dog will do a Ring Procedure Broad Jump with medium proofing: ☐ _____ [ ]
    a) Another person is talking to the dog before he is sent.
    b) Another person is tempting the dog to come to them when he lands over the jump.
    c) The dog's back is facing the jump.

17. The dog will do the Ring Procedure Broad Jump with heavy proofing: ☐ _____ [ ]
    a) Another person is offering food or petting the dog before the handler sends the dog.
    b) Another person is throwing a ball or toy out in front of the dog to prevent him from turning and sitting front, after he jumps.

RETRIEVE

STEPS: COMPLETED   DATE   COMMENTS

1. The dog in heel position will allow the handler to open his mouth by applying pressure to his lips and place the dumbbell in his mouth just behind the lower canine teeth. The dog does not fight having the dumbbell in his mouth.   ☐   _____   _____

2. The dog will voluntarily open his mouth upon feeling the pressure of the dumbbell on his teeth and accept the dumbbell into his mouth. The handler knows how to ear pinch correctly and is ready if the dog doesn't open his mouth to accept the dumbbell.   ☐   _____   _____

3. The dog will allow the handler to gently push his head to the dumbbell placed 1" in front of the dog's mouth. The handler uses the ear pinch only if the dog doesn't open his mouth upon feeling the dumbbell on his lips (step 2.) The dog is still sitting in heel position.   ☐   _____   _____

4. The dog will reach one inch for the dumbbell or command without the ear pinch. The handler is ready to pinch if needed.   ☐   _____   _____

5. The dog will reach six inches for the dumbbell, held at eye level with surrounding distractions. The handler is ready to pinch if needed.   ☐   _____   _____

Retrieve...Cont'.

STEPS: COMPLETED   DATE   COMMENTS

6. The dog will reach 1 foot for the dumbbell at eye level, below eye level and above eye level. Since the dog has to stand and move forward to reach the dumbbell, the handler gives the "come" command and moves backwards to help the dog sit front holding the dumbbell. The handler's right hand prevents the dumbbell from falling out of the dog's mouth as the dog comes to sit front. ☐ _____

7. The dog will hold the dumbbell without chewing or mouthing it for 1 minute while sitting in front position. The handler prevents the dog from dropping the dumbbell by gently holding the dog's mouth closed. ☐ _____

8. The dog will retrieve the dumbbell from the floor with the handler's hand on it. The dumbbell is placed with only one end touching the floor. ☐ _____

9. The dog will do step # 8 with just one of the handler's fingers on the dumbbell. The dumbbell is completely on the floor. The handler closes the dog's mouth from under his chin if necessary. ☐ _____

10. The dog will do step # 8 with the handler pointing to the dumbbell (the handler's finger is close to the dumbbell.) ☐ _____

11. The dog will do step # 10 with the handler standing up and pointing to the dumbbell. ☐ _____

12. The dog will do steps # 1 through # 11 with the handler holding the ear. ☐ _____

Retrieve...Cont'.

STEPS: COMPLETED   DATE   COMMENTS

13. The dog will hold the dumbbell while standing and move with the
    dumbbell in his mouth. The dog understands he will get an ear pinch
    if he drops the dumbbell.   ☐   ____   ☐

14. The dog will retrieve the dumbbell a leash length away off the ground
    and return and sit front. The dog is sent as the dumbbell hits the
    ground and told to come as he picks up the dumbbell.   ☐   ____   ☐

15. The dog will do step #14 with distractions (e.g. food, another dog,
    other animals, different locations.)   ☐   ____   ☐

16. The dog will hold the sit stay on lead while the dumbbell is tossed a
    leash length away and on the command "take it" will retrieve the
    dumbbell and turn and come sit front.   ☐   ____   ☐

17. The dog will do step #16 with distractions (same type used in step #15).
    The dog is still on lead.   ☐   ____   ☐

RETRIEVE on FLAT

STEPS:	COMPLETED	DATE	COMMENTS

1. Having been taught a forced retrieve, the dog will reliably and confidently retrieve the dumbbell thrown a leash length away and come sit front.

2. The dog on a long line will retrieve the dumbbell from a sit stay position, on the "take it" command when the dumbbell is thrown 10' away.

3. The dog will do step # 2 with light proofing (e.g. other person or animal near the dumbbell or different locations.)

4. The dog will do step # 2 with moderate proofing (e.g. other person talking to the dog, the dumbbell thrown on different surfaces or different weather conditions. The dumbbell thrown under a chair or up on a step.)

5. The dog will do step # 2 with heavy proofing (e.g. other person offering food or petting the dog, two dogs retrieving at the same time, the dumbbell is up on it's end. The dumbbell landing near food or toys.)

6. The dog will do step # 2 with the dumbbell thrown 20 feet.

7. The dog will do step # 2 with light, moderate and heavy proofing (use same type of proofs used for 10'.)

8. The dog will retrieve on command a leash length off lead and will come sit front.

Retrieve on flat....Cont'

STEPS:	COMPLETED	DATE	COMMENTS

9. The dog will do step # 8 with light proofing (e.g. same light proofing discussed earlier.) ☐ ____

10. The dog will do step # 8 with moderate proofing (e.g. same moderate proofing discussed earlier.) ☐ ____

11. The dog will do step # 8 with heavy proofing (e.g. same heavy proofing discussed earlier.) ☐ ____

12. The dog will retrieve the dumbbell thrown 10 feet off lead. ☐ ____

13. The dog will do step # 12 with light proofing (e.g. proofing used for leash length.) ☐ ____

14. The dog will do step # 12 with moderate proofing (e.g. same used for leash length.) ☐ ____

15. The dog will do step # 12 with heavy proofing (e.g. same proofing used for leash length.) ☐ ____

16. The dog will retrieve the dumbbell thrown 20 feet. ☐ ____

17. The dog will do step # 16 with light proofing. ☐ ____

18. The dog will do step # 16 with moderate proofing. ☐ ____

19. The dog will do step # 16 with heavy proofing. ☐ ____

20. The dog will do ring procedure retrieve on flat with confidence. ☐ ____

DROP ON RECALL

COMPLETED   DATE   COMMENTS

STEPS:

1. The dog will down in motion confidently (step 2 in <u>Beyond Basic Dog Training</u> page 131)

2. The dog will do windmill down (step 3 page 133)

3. The dog on 6' lead will do Comefore and drop on verbal command only. The dog understands to drop only on the word "Down" and to ignore other word said by the handler.

4. The dog will do step #3 and down only on the handler's "Down" command, ignoring other people's commands to down.

5. The dog on 6' lead will do Comefore and drop on signal only and understands to ignore all of the handler's extraneous body language.

6. The dog will do step #5 and down on only the handler's signal, ignoring other people's signals.

7. The dog will maintain attention after being dropped as the handler backs away to the end of the 6' lead. The dog is released with "Okay" and encouraged to come to the handler enthusiastically.

8. The dog will do a formal recall and drop briskly and correctly on command approximately 6' in front of the handler dropping before the handler touches the dog. The handler walks to the dog immediately following the command. The dog is released with "Okay" and encouraged to jump up on the handler.

Drop ... cont.'

STEPS: COMPLETED   DATE   COMMENTS

9. The dog will do step #8 being dropped 10' in front of the handler.
   The Handler walks in to meet the dog.   ☐

10. The dog will do step #8 being dropped 15' in front of the handler.
    The Handler walks in to meet the dog.   ☐

11. The dog will down on command confidently. After walking to the dog
    following "Down", the handler backs up, keeping the dog's attention,
    and gives the dog a Come command.   ☐

12. The dog will drop briskly on command without the handler walking into
    the dog and comes briskly off the down to sit front.   ☐

13. The dog will do a confident drop on recall with light proofing:
    a) Someone playing Judge.
    b) Proofs used for comefore drop which are in Steps 4 and 6.   ☐

14. The dog will do confident drop on recall with moderate proofing:
    a) The dog will drop on different surfaces.
    b) The dog will do exercise with the handler on knees.
    c) The dog understands difference between straight recall and drop. Will
       do either with confidence no matter how many repetitions of each are done.
    d) The dog will do a drop with the judge following close behind on the recall.

DIRECTED JUMPING

STEPS:	COMPLETED	DATE	COMMENTS

1. The dog will jump on hand signal only and body language a bar or high jump set at 1/3 the dog's jump height. The handler sets up either 2 bars or 2 high jumps with a gate between the jumps. The dog and handler are both 8' back from the center of the gate. ☐

2. The dog will jump either direction on hand signal only with the jumps set 10' apart and the gate removed. The dog and handler are approximately 15' from the center. ☐

3. The dog will jump either direction on hand signal only with a bar and a high jump set up 18 – 20' apart. The dog and handler are both at full distance. The jump height is still set low. ☐

4. The dog will do step #3 with light proofing. (i.e., The handler walking over one jump and sending the dog over the other. The handler leaning one way and giving the signal to the other jump.) ☐

5. The dog will do step #3 with moderate proofing. (i.e., Someone else taps the jumps and you send to the other jump. Set the jumps 30' apart and someone else is talking to your dog before you give the signal.) ☐

6. The dog will do step #3 with heavy proofing. (i.e., Someone throws a ball or other distractions in front of your dog as he heads for the jump. Stand with your back to the dog and give the signal. Give the signal on your knees.) ☐

7. The dog (not puppies or young dogs), will do the exercise with the jumps set at full height without distractions. Gradually raise the jump heights for full grown dogs only. ☐

8. The dog will do step #7 with distractions. ☐

DIRECTED RETRIEVE

	COMPLETED	DATE	COMMENTS

STEPS:

1. The dog will retrieve a stuffed glove on a verbal command without mouthing or shaking it.

2. The handler can give a correct hand signal without the dog (page 179 of Beyond Basic Dog Training.)

3. The dog understands that the hand signal means to look for a glove. When the hand signal is given, the dog looks past the signal and retrieves on command a tossed glove.

4. The dog demonstrates understanding of the difference between a retrieve and directed retrieve. With the dog sitting in "Heel Position" facing #2 glove (no glove there) the dog will look on the hand signal at #1 and 3, and will retrieve either glove on command. The dog is on a long line and the gloves are tossed approximately 8 feet.

5. The dog will do step #4 with the handler tossing the glove 15'.

6. The dog will retrieve either the #1 or #3 glove with the center glove (#2) added (2 ft. closer) The dog is on a long line facing #2 glove and the gloves are placed approximately 10' away. The dog isn't sent to #2.

7. The handler can pivot correctly to each glove without the dog.

Directed Retrieve ... cont.

STEPS:　　　　　　　　　　　　　　　　　COMPLETED　DATE　COMMENTS

8. The handler and dog can pivot correctly to each glove and the dog will retrieve the glove he was pivoted to. The gloves are placed 20' away and no longer stuffed and the dog is off lead. ☐

9. The dog will retrieve the correct glove with light proofing, e.g.,
   a) The dog is pivoted to one glove an sent to another.
   b) The #2 glove is placed 5' closer to the dog and handler and the dog sent to #1 or #3.
   c) The dog will do the glove exercise in three (3) different locations. ☐

10. The dog will retrieve the correct glove with moderate proofing:
    a) The #2 glove is placed 5' further away from the dog and handler than #1 or #3 and the dog is sent to #2.
    b) The gloves are placed in high grass.
    c) Using colored gloves that match the terrain.
    d) Another person talking to the dog when he is retrieving the glove.
    e) A glove is tossed in front of the dog as he is sent to retrieve a glove to see if he will switch gloves mid–way in retrieve. ☐

11. The dog will retrieve the correct glove with heavy proofing:
    a) Another person offering food to the dog while he is retrieving.
    b) Two dogs doing gloves at the same time, either same set of gloves or two sets.
    c) The dog can do directed retrieve with 6 – 8 gloves in a circle (make sure signal is clear). ☐

MOVING STAND

STEPS:	COMPLETED	DATE	COMMENTS

1. The dog understands the Novice Stand Signal and can stand on signal only from a sit in heel position. ☐ _____ ☐

2. While heeling, the dog will stand in heel position when the handler gives a verbal stand command and signal. ☐ _____ ☐

3. The dog can do step # 2 with the stand signal only. ☐ _____ ☐

4. The dog will stand and stay in heel position when the handler gives the stand signal and verbal stay command. The handler uses correct footwork when leaving the dog to walk 10 – 12 feet away and turn and face the dog. ☐ _____ ☐

5. The dog will stand motionless while the "Judge" examines him. ☐ _____ ☐

6. The dog will come directly to heel position from a sit 3 feet in front of the handler on lead with help from the handler. The handler helps by guiding the dog around with the leash. ☐ _____ ☐

7. The dog will do step # 6 without help from the handler. ☐ _____ ☐

8. From a sit, 3 feet in front of the handler, the dog will, on command and signal to "heel" will go directly to heel position. ☐ _____ ☐

9. The dog can do the same exercise from a stand position. ☐ _____ ☐

10. The dog can do the exercise when the distance is increased. ☐ _____ ☐

11. The dog can do the entire exercise correctly with confidence. ☐ _____ ☐

SCENT DISCRIMINATION

STEPS: COMPLETED   DATE   COMMENTS

1. The dog will retrieve willingly and with distractions, off the floor, the leather and metal articles (ones with no numbers on them or "0" or "6"). ☐

2. On the command "Take It!", the dog will go to the board and find the metal article NOT TIED down and bring it back and sit front. The dog is on a 6' lead and facing the article board in heel position. There are only 2 tied down metal articles at this stage. ☐

3. The dog will do step #2 with the command "Find It!". ☐

4. The dog will do the exercise starting with his back toward the board. The handler puts down the article. On "Heel" command the dog will turn around with the handler and sit in heel position. On the command "Find It!" the dog will leave the handler and go work the board. The dog may not be scenting yet. ☐

5. The dog will do step 4 with 2 more tied down articles with confidence. The dog should be scenting now. If not, refer to the chapter in <u>Beyond Basic Dog Training.</u> ☐

6. The dog will do step 5 with another person acting as the steward and the Judge putting out the article. ☐

Scenting.... Cont.

STEPS:	COMPLETED	DATE	COMMENTS

7. The dog will do the exercise when the steward (friend) has touched each of the tied down articles. The dog is on leash. ☐

8. The dog will do step 7 off leash. ☐

9. The dog will do step 7 having at least 10 other people touch the tied down articles. Of course only have one other scent on the tied down articles at a time. ☐

10. The dog will do step 7 off lead still only 6' away with distractions around the board. i.e., noises, people, other dogs, food. Proofing begins light and increases as the dog understands to keep his mind on his job. ☐

11. The dog will do step 10, 15' away scenting with confidence while being proofed. ☐

12. The dog will do steps 2 through 11 with the leather articles. ☐

13. The dog will do step 3 through 10 (except with no distractions) with 3 metal and 3 leather articles tied down. The handler alternates sending the dog for a metal and a leather article. The handler is consistent with which article he sends the dog for first and doesn't repeat a correct retrieve. ☐

14. The dog will do step 13 with distractions. ☐

15. The dog will do the exercise correctly with 1 metal article retied on a 6" string that allows the article to be placed off the board. No distractions at this point. ☐

Scenting.... Cont.

STEPS: COMPLETED   DATE   COMMENTS

16. The dog will do step 15 with a leather article also on a 6" string. ☐ ____ ☐

17. The dog will do the exercise correctly regardless of where the scented article is placed. (on or off board). ☐ ____ ☐

18. The dog will scent correctly with 2 metal and 2 leather articles on 6" strings with distractions. ☐ ____ ☐

19. The dog will do the exercise correctly with all the articles tied on 6" strings and most of them placed off the board with distractions. ☐ ____ ☐

20. The dog will do the exercise correctly without the board, using only 2 metal and 2 leather articles in the pile. ☐ ____ ☐

21. The dog will do step 20 with the correct number of articles and with confidence. ☐ ____ ☐

22. The dog will do the exercise correctly with proofing. i.e., 20 articles in a pile, articles placed on different surfaces, with a fan blowing on them all kinds of weather, different locations, articles placed in different patterns on the floor, ball or bone in the pile. ☐ ____ ☐

SIGNAL EXERCISE

STEPS: COMPLETED DATE COMMENTS

1. The dog will heel with attention off lead. The handler knows how to give the correct Utility hand signals. (Practice in front of a mirror without the dog.) ☐ _____

2. The dog will heel with attention on lead, after being given the heel command and signal. ☐ _____

3. The dog will heel with attention on lead, after being given only the hand signal. Remember to praise verbally. ☐ _____

4. The dog will do step #3 with proofing, (i.e. talking to the dog, petting the dog, offering food when the handler gives the heel signal.) ☐ _____

5. The dog will do step #4 off lead. ☐ _____

6. While heeling on lead, the dog will stand in heel position on signal only. (The Utility stand signal is the Novice stand signal the dog already learned.) ☐ _____

7. The dog will do step #6 with proofing, (i.e., someone talking to the dog, petting the dog, offering food, someone playing "Judge" giving multiple stand commands.) ☐ _____

8. The dog will drop in place on a 6' lead from a stand on signal only. (The "down" hand signal is the same as the drop on recall hand signal.) ☐ _____

9. The dog will do step #7 with proofing, (i.e. talking to the dog, petting the dog, offering food when the handler gives the heel signal.) ☐ _____

Signals.... Cont.

STEPS: COMPLETED   DATE   COMMENTS

10. The dog will sit on hand signal only on a 6' lead from a sphinx down. (The dog's front feet must move backwards to meet the back feet so that the dog sits in place.)

11. The dog will do step #10 with proofing.

12. The dog will come from a sit on a 6' lead with a modified Karate Chop recall signal. (See the chapter on Signals in <u>Beyond Basic Dog Training</u>)

13. The dog will do step #12 with proofing.

14. The dog can do a drop, sit and come off lead 6' away confidently and correctly.

15. The dog can do step #14 on lead with some proofing.

16. The dog can do step #14 ring distance. (Distance reached slowly.) Proofing is done at each new distance.

17. The dog will finish with a verbal command and signal on the lead.

18. The dog will do step #17 with signal only.

19. The dog can do step #18 with proofing.

20. The dog can finish on signal only off lead, with proofing.

21. The dog can do the entire ring procedure signal exercise with proofing.

147

GO OUT

STEPS: COMPLETED   DATE   COMMENTS

1. The dog will allow himself to be pulled 6' to a barrier into chutes with the handler walking behind and pointing Go-Out with the right hand. The dog will stand with his nose touching the barrier. The handler walks to the Go-Out target pointing before sending the dog. On "Okay" the dog is turned in the chutes to encourage a tight turn later on.   ☐   _____   ☐

2. The dog will allow himself to be pulled out from 6' outside of the chutes to the target into the chutes without the handler moving. Handler still points out Go-Out to the target spot on the gates before sending the dog.   ☐   _____   ☐

3. The dog will do step #2 from 15' outside of the chutes.   ☐

4. The dog will go confidently into the chutes on command from 15' away without puller having to use any pressure on the line. The handler's still pointing out target before sending the dog and following the dog to praise him for standing with his nose touching the barrier.   ☐   _____   ☐

5. The dog will Go-Out on command off lead and stand at the gate from 6' outside of the chutes. The handler still points out Go-Out target before standing the dog. The handler follows the dog to physically praise the dog at the Go-Out.   ☐   _____   ☐

6. The dog will do step #5 from 15' outside of the chutes.   ☐

Go—Out .... cont'

STEPS: COMPLETED   DATE   COMMENTS

7. The dog will Go—Out on command through guides to the gate target off lead from 15' outside of the chutes. The guides one used to teach the dog to Go straight. The handler only points out the first Go-Out, but still the dog to make sure the dog stands facing the barrier. ☐

8. The dog will Go—Out on command from 6' outside of the chutes and turns and sits in the chutes on command. The handler follows the dog to prevent the dog from walking forward on sit command. The handler points out the first Go—Out if it's an unfamiliar area. ☐

9. The dog will do step #8 from 15' outside of the chutes. ☐

10. The dog will go out full distance through the guides and turns and sit on command in the chutes that have been reduced to size of rulers. The handler still points out the first Go-Out in an unfamiliar area. ☐

11. The dog will do step #10 with light proofing. e.g.
a) People and dogs standing and moving behind the barrier. ☐

12. The dog will do step#10 with moderate proofing:
a) Someone talking to, petting or offering food to the dog before he is sent.
b) Someone throwing a ball or toy in front of the dog doing a Go-Out.
c) Someone talking to the dog while he is heading for the Go—Our target. ☐

13. The dog will Go—Out and turn and sit in the chutes from 6' outside of the guides to different barriers, (e.g. solid wall, string gate, fences. The handler points out the first Go—Out, the handler is no longer walking toward the dog.) ☐

Go–Out .... cont'

STEPS:	COMPLETED	DATE	COMMENTS

14. The dog will do step #13 from full distance.

15. The dog will do full distance Go–Out, through 3 sets of chutes (last set 3' from Go–Out barrier) and turn and sit in any set of chutes on command.

16. The dog will do full distance Go–Out with chutes gradually being taken away. The handler only points out Go–Out the first time.

17. The dog will do short Go–Out (6') without chutes or the handler pointing out Go–Out target. The dog finds Go–Out by himself.

18. The dog will do step #17 full distance.

19. The dog will do full distance Go–Out without the chutes or help from the handler with light proofing (see Step #11).

20. The dog will do step #19 with moderate proofing. (see Step #12).

21. The dog will do step #19 with heavy proofing. (e.g. The handler throws the ball into a corner of the ring, then command "Go–Out", without dog watching, have someone place crumbled pieces of paper in corners (that resemble gloves) and send the dog on Go–Out.) Do three (3) glove retrieves and than a Go–Out for glove retrieve.)

A DAY AT THE SHOW

or
"Tomorrow will be a better day"

The following is a fictional account of one handler's "Day at the show". After reading through the scenario, list below all the things that could have been done differently to improve their dog's performance

Linda and her yellow dog Chester walked into the air-conditioned show site at a local trial. She was a bit nervous because Chester was 6th in the Utility ring and this was his first attempt at a leg. Linda looked at her watch – 9:00 am. Good, the show had just started. She set up her crate and chair and noticed a fellow club member sitting at the other end of the building. Hastily she gave Chester his breakfast and hurried over with him to greet her friend. Feeling that she had plenty of time she chatted nervously about the days events, and then, remembers that she had to "Check–in", ran with Chester to the ring steward and got her armband. Linda had been told by a "seasoned" Utility person that if she was sixth in the ring she could expect an hour wait. Linda had carefully planned that she and Chester would be at the ringside, warmed up and ready at 10:00 on the dot. She ran him outside for a quick potty break and resumed her conversation with her friend. Much to her surprise, about 15 minutes later, she heard the ring steward calling out her number. Leaving Chester with her friend, she walked over to see what he wanted.

As it turned out, it was her and Chester that they wanted! She was next in the ring! Linda told the steward that this could not be the case because she was sixth and that meant she should be in around 10:00. The steward replied that the 2nd, 3rd, and 4th dog had not signed in, so she was next. Linda raced over to the now sleeping Chester, ran back to her crate, got her article bag, searched for her gloves, and threw them in the bag with her articles. Nearly out of breath, Linda and Chester arrived at ringside. Fortunately, the judge was sympathetic, kind and politely invited Linda into the ring.

As the judge measured Chester, he noticed the collar Chester was wearing was a nylon collar with a plastic "Quick Release" clip on it. He told Linda that this type of collar was not allowed, and to please leave the ring and return with a regulation collar. Linda, by this time near hysterics, looked over at her friend and frantically motioned her over to the ring. Minutes passed, and her friend came over to the ring and gave Linda a choke chain. Relieved, she slipped the collar on the dog and entered the ring (again) to begin her class.

As the judge began calling the heeling commands, Linda realized that she hadn't seen the pattern. Not to worry, she thought, I can just listen. Thinking quickly, Linda realized that a halt hadn't been given yet. She began slowing down in anticipation of a halt, when much to her surprise, the judge called a "Fast" and Chester (anticipating her cue to halt, or at least to go slow) lagged considerably. Mercifully, the judge called normal, then a turn followed by a "Stand your dog." Linda left Chester on a stand, and walked briskly to the other end of the ring. Turning around she awaited the judges signal.

The judge flashed her a quick signal to drop the dog. Much to Chester's surprise, Linda flashed him a quick signal that he thought he saw, yet, in practice her signals were much more even and fluid, so he didn't stop, thinking she had just flinched (which was what it looked like). Linda scowled at him, and the judge motioned her to give him another signal. This time Linda gave her usual signal and Chester dropped confidently (not sure why she was scowling). The sit and come signals executed perfectly (by both dog and handler) and they were now ready for articles.

The judge handed Linda two #4 articles and she turned herself and the dog and scented the articles. At this point the nice judge began a long discussion with Linda about the merits of flying non-stop into the city. This provided a lovely opportunity for Chester to take a nap while sitting. Just as Chester was dreaming the part in his dream where he almost catches the rabbit, Linda abruptly stuck her hand in front of his nose and said "Heel." Chester's body works like that of a dog who has been sleeping and he moves at a slow crawl through the pivot. Linda looked at him and scowled again. "Find it," she said harshly, and Chester, who has a full tummy from breakfast, and just recently awakened from a nap, took a nice ling scratch before going out to the pile. Darn those fleas - it has been a long time, after all, since he has had a bath. After a scratch, Chester walked out to the pile. All the articles smelled like Linda! In fact, more specifically, they all smelled like her gloves! thinking that this is easier than he remembered, Chester picked up the first glove-like smelling article and trots (a stretch for him in his post-nap state) happily back to her. Linda scowls as she took the article. Hmmmm. As Linda scented the next article, it was nap time again as she discussed with the judge her dog's bad attitude. Once again, the second article goes much like the first. Scowl.

Next Linda sets up for gloves. This is her ace in the hole! Chester loves gloves and has never failed in practice. The judge told her "Glove #1." Due to Linda's confidence, she gave Chester an impressively quick signal simultaneous with an impressively quick "Fetch" command. Chester (locked in on glove #2) impressively ducked under her hand and retrieved glove #2. Boy, does he love gloves!. Racing back he notices her scowl. Reluctantly Chester gives Linda the glove, and just for fun jumps up on her and gives her a big kiss! Linda smiles and hugs Chester - after all he is cute, so she plays with him all the way to the place where the judge wants her to begin the moving stand.

Now Chester is even more hyped than before. The actual stand and exam part go well. But on the heel, Chester gets another flea attack and walks in, stops to scratch, walks in, then stops and scratches again. This continued until he finally makes it into heel position. Linda sighs. This has been the longest day of her life!

Only Go-Outs are left. Linda sends her dog and Chester runs back, heading directly for the corner where glove #1 was. Linda waits until Chester has gone into the corner and then yells for him to sit. He does and Linda commands, "Bar." Chester races over and jumps the bar and then goes directly to heel. Linda is so happy that he took the correct jump and went all the way out that she releases him, hugs him, and plays with him until the judge taps her on the shoulder and reminds her that there are two parts to this exercise. Linda tries to get the near frenzied Chester into some semblance of heel position and, on the judges orders, sends him out again. Linda yells "Sit," but Chester is too hyped to sit, and since she loved his last bar jump, he races towards and soars over the bar jump again, expecting to run into open arms! Scowl. Oh well, he thinks, Tomorrow will be a better day.

The judge tells Linda that Chester needs more practice, but not to give up.

LIST OF THINGS TO IMPROVE LINDA AND CHESTER'S PERFORMANCE

1. Linda could have arrived at the show earlier. Just because her entry said she would have been 6th in the ring does not necessarily mean she will be (as she found out).

2. Depending on the type of dog, feeding the dog so close to "show" time can be detrimental. Not all dogs work well on full stomachs.

3. Depending on the dog, running him around the show site can tire out or wire up a dog. Many dogs do well confined to their crates before showing.

4. Putting gloves in your article bag will contaminate the articles. All of them! Store gloves separately, please.

5. Know the rules. This includes rules on the type of collars allowed in the ring. Plain buckle collars and chokes are allowed.

6. Never anticipate ANYTHING! Even if Linda had known there was a halt in a certain spot, should have waited until the called it. She miscued Chester by hesitating.

7. Just because the judge flashed her a signal did not mean she should flash Chester his signal! Linda should try not to get flustered and remember to think about what she is going to do before she does it!

8. Never show the dog you are upset with him in the ring. Fortunately, Chester was only puzzled by Linda's scowling, but some dogs will get very upset and this will cause them to be stressed on the other exercises. Being disappointed is understandable, but don't let the dog feel you are angry with him.

List...Cont'.

9. While scenting your article, if the judge should wish to engage in conversation please don't forget about the dog! Linda should have been paying attention to Chester, talking to him, perhaps giving him a little scratch under the chin, anything to let him know that she was still alive, they were still in a work mode, and that she would appreciate his participation!

10. Always bring a clean dog to a show. The dog feels better, the judges (who have to touch the dog) will feel better, and you won't have to worry about fleas attacking the dog during a crucial part of the run—through!

11. As for the article problem goes, see #4.

12. No matter how well the dog does gloves, since you are permitted to give a slow, careful signal take advantage of that! You should not try to impress anyone. If Linda had given her signal and command separately (as opposed to her simultaneous version), she may have seen Chester's eyes on #2, and perhaps delayed her verbal, waiting to see if he would look where she was directing him to.

13. Remember the advise that you should not act angry towards the dog who NQ's. You should also not exuberantly reinforce the incorrect behavior by praising wildly, hugging and kissing the dog. A simple release, with a few softly spoken words of encouragement mean a lot.

14. If you have a dog who tends to get hyped up for a particular exercise, don't encourage him into a hyped up frenzy. Speak calmly and softly to him. Doing run—through's with someone who has a good understanding of the rules and regulations can help you prepare for the "real — thing". This cannot make up for having a dog who hasn't been trained sufficiently enough qualify. Correction matches are great "dress rehearsals" and the fact that you may correct if needed, will make you feel more in control.

LIST OF THINGS TO BRING TO A DOG SHOW

1. Your dog (don't laugh, it's happened!)
2. Leash and regulation collar without tags.
3. Crate and crate mat.
4. Water bowl and water.
5. Plastic bags to pick up after your dog
   (size of the bag depends on the size of the dog)
6. Chair.
7. A cooler with food and drinks for you
   (and your friends)
8. Copy of the AKC Obedience Rules and Regulations.
9. Obedience trial record book
   (if you have one)
10. Pen
    (actually, two or three as this is a popularly borrowed and not returned item!)
11. Sun screen and hat if at an outdoor show.
12. Video camera and tape — or just a tape if you have a friend with a camera.
13. Flea spray and/or powder.
14. A spouse or significant other to help carry it all!
15. Good sportsmanship and a sense of humor!

WHERE TO GO FOR TRAINING HELP

Okay, you want to do very well in obedience (or just qualify!) and you don't know where to turn for help. Take heart, there is always a way to achieve your goal.

Read the list below and then START training!

1. First, look into a local training club.
   DO NOT bring your dog to the first class you observe.
   Make sure the method and philosophy agree with your own. Watch the more advanced level classes. Talk to the people participating and get their feelings about the training. If possible, go to a show and observe the students (and instructors) in the ring. Watch for the types of warm-ups they use, the performance of the dog in the ring and how the handler handles him in the ring. After an NQ performance, watch the handler's reaction to the dog *outside* the ring.

2. No club nearby? There are many books and videos out that can help you in the comfort of your own home! Just by reading this book you have started on the road to improvement!

3. Go to a seminar or camp. Many seminars and camps give hands-on help for your specific problem.

4. Train by video tape. Sending a tape to a trainer whose method you are familiar and comfortable with (and hopefully you are using the method) can be very helpful. Usually trainers charge an hourly fee to watch and write a critique for the tape. If you want a phone consultation, phone charges will usually be reversed, or you will call at a prearranged time.

5. Train by phone. If you can accurately describe the problem, call a trainer who does phone consultations. They may be able to accurately diagnose and suggest solutions to problems you may be having. Again an hourly rate will apply, and you should be familiar and comfortable with this trainer's methods (because after all, that is what you will be asked to apply as a solution!)

THE ANSWERS TO ALL YOUR QUESTIONS!

INCLUDING ......

MATCH SHOW LOGS !
and
PERSONAL NOTE AREAS!

---- ANSWERS ----

Page 3

1. NO
2. YES
3. NO
4. YES
5. NO
6. YES
7. NO
8. YES
9. YES
10. NO

Page 8

1. Training
2. Show
3. Training
4. Show
5. Training
6. Show
7. Show
8. Show

Page 9/10

1. – D
2. – B
3. – A, B, C, E
4. – D, I, D, D, I, I

Page 11/12

1. – Hard Eyes – Focused on the dog's head.
2. – Hard Eyes – Focused on where you want the dog's rear to end up.
3. – Soft Eyes – Relaxed
4. – Soft Eyes – Must be the same as #5 or it will not carry over into a ring situation.
5. – Soft Eyes – So you can see the judge.
6. – Hard Eyes – To help direct the dog to the glove. The dog will see you looking at the glove.
7. – Hard Eyes – To help direct the dog to the pile.
8. – Hard Eyes – To help direct the dog to go out.
9. – Soft Eyes – So the dog focuses on your hand signal and not your eyes.
10. – Hard Eyes – To help show the dog where to look.
11. – Hard Eyes – To help direct the dog back over the jump.
12. – Soft Eyes – So as not to encourage the dog to come to you. The dog must be thinking jump, not about getting to you.
13. – Hard Eyes – To encourage focus and attention.
14. – Soft Eyes – So as not to threaten by changing to Hard Eyes if the dog starts to break.
15. – Hard Eyes – To maintain focus and attention throughout exam.

Page 13

1. – T
2. – F
3. – F
4. – T
5. – T
6. – F (They usually like them more – less competition.)
7. – T (Specialty awards for specific breeds.)
8. – T
9. – F (Get a better definition of failure)
10. – F (Not if their trainer improves.)

Page 14

You should have put a line through numbers 3, 4, 5 and 9.

Answers...cont'.

Page 22/23
1. C
2. B, C, D   E. – would be considered an aid to the dog.
   A. – is not possible for most dogs if they are in correct heel position and the handler is looking straight ahead.
3. F   It is exactly the same.
4. F   Not if they are trained to look at your left side, instead of your eyes.
5. F   Any part of the dog that interferes with the handler's leg can be considered crowding.
6. F   Dogs must change pace, not gait. Most small dogs do break into a canter from a trot.
7. T
8. F   It is to the dog's advantage but it is not a rule. Sometimes you can't help but stop on your left foot.
9. T   Which is why you should practice long slows, and long fasts.
10. T
11. F   You practice on leash heeling the entire career of the dog. On leash heeling helps define heel position.
12. F   If you don't practice off leash heeling, you will never get good at it.
13. T
14. F   Only a tight leash helps define heel position.
15. T   The dog doesn't have to slow down as much to maintain heel position.

Page 27
1 – E 2. – D

Page 31/32
1. – Forward
2. – Halt
3. – Right Turn
4. – Fast
5. – About Turn
6. – Send your dog
7. – Throw it.
8. – Leave your dog.

Answers...Cont'.

Page 33

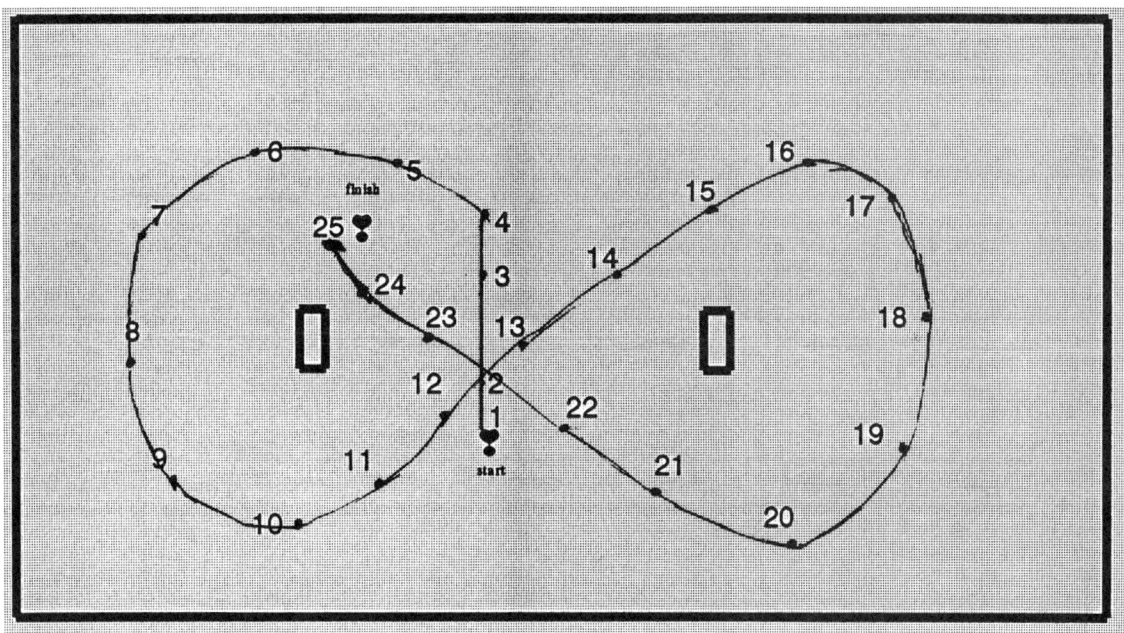

Page 34/35
Match Game: 1. – B, 2. – C, 3. – D, 4. – A, 5. – F, 6. – E
Order of Teaching: 1. – C, 2. – A, 3. – B, 4. – E, 5. – D

Answers...cont'.

Page 36
1. – T   Be sure to introduce the stick to the dog using it as a training tool.
2. – F   The key to the finish is teaching the dog to move around behind you with his head up.
           The dog who goes way behind you is not moving efficiently into heel position and is likely to get distracted.
3. – T
4. – F   BIG – dogs may require two steps.
5. – T
6. – F   Dogs take longer to learn the finish because you are asking them to do series of things on one command.

Page 37
1. – E & F   4. – D   7. – G
2. – B   5. – A
3. – C   6. – H

Page 38
1. – T   2. – F   Stepping back teaches a dog to get closer. When a dog is too close to you he must bend
                   his spine which cause a crooked sit. Most handlers step back and in front of the dog so
                   they end up doing all the adjusting. Thus the dog learns nothing about how to straighten a front.
3. – T   4. – F   Dogs with short backs are easier to teach to sit straight.
5. – T   6. – F   A rocked back sit will often place the dog too far from the handler in the sit – front position.
7. – T   8. – F   The dog should be looking for front which will be on your midline slightly above his eye level.
                   As the dog bends into a sit he may look higher (to your face) but he uses the lower spot
                   to line up the sit.
9. – F   They should be taught to look at the space between your legs if they are short enough to do this and look
          up. The trainer's feet should be close together so the dog's body can block the handler's feet.
10. – T
11. – T
12. – T
13. – F   It teaches the dog to do nothing and wait for you to move him.
          He has no idea where he is or how he got there.
14. – T

Page 39/40
1. – N, M   5. – M   9. – S
2. – N, S, M   6. – N, M   10. – N
3. – S, M   7. – N   11. – M
4. – N, M   8. – M   12. – S

Page 41
a. – 2   d. – 3   g. – 4
b. – 5   e. – 6   h. – 7
c. – 8   f. – 1   i. – 9

Page 46
I. – c   Height doesn't make it easier. If you push the
       return to sit front, you encourage him to cut
       the corner.
II. – c
III. – a & c (this will cause him to cut the corner even more!)
IV. – e

Answers...cont'

Page 47/48
- I.   A #1, B #2, C #3
- II.   So the dog does not get to see gloves one and two as he turns.
- III.   B & D   V. — B
- IV.   C & D   VI. — A

Page 52

Answers...Cont'

Page 54/55

1. – A & B	3. – A	5. – B	7. – B & C	9. – B & C
2. – C & B	4. – B	6. – C	8. – B	

Page 56

1. – T
2. – F (unless the dog is very small)
3. – T
4. – T
5. – T
6. – T
7. – T
8. – F
9. – T
10. – T
11. – T
12. – F
13. – T
14. – T

Page 57/58

1	A	9	V	17	O, V
2	K, A, O, V	10	O, V	18	V
3	A, V	11	V, K	19	V
4	V, K	12	A, V	20	V
5	O, V	13	V, K		
6	V	14	V		
7	A, V	15	V		
8	O, V	16	A		

Page 60 – ANSWERS:

Answers:
1) A. Leave the dog on a sit-stay and ask someone else (non family member) to go over to the dog and say, "down!" If the dog still sits, have the family member point to the floor and say, "down!"
   B. Put the dog on a sit-stay on your bed. Get into bed and turn the lights off. Wait. (Be sure you don't fall asleep before the dog lies down!)
   C. Do a sit-stay and have someone come to your front door and ring the door bell. Answer the door. Greet your friend. If the dog is still staying, sit down and talk with your friend. Be sure to keep one eye on the dog waiting for a mistake.
2) A. Tell your dog to finish and have someone standing behind you with food, a toy or just petting and talking to the dog so that the dog gets distracted. Now you are in a position to correct a slow finish.
3) A. Throw the dumbbell off to the side.
   B. Drape a jacket on the jump or tie balloons to the uprights to make the jump look scary.
   C. Stand with the dog in heel position at the end of the jump so the dog has to angle his movement to go over the jump.

   D. Have a person walk across the jump on the other side as you command the dog to jump.

   E. Set up two high jumps 12 feet apart and throw the dumbbell over both jumps.
4) A. Put a long line on the dog and as you say, "Stay", leave on your right foot and put gentle pressure on the long line. If the dog gets up, you will feel it and be in a position to correct.
   B. If the dog is sitting as you turn to face him for the recall, call his name only. If he gets up, put him back. A dog should not get up on his name for any command and will be scored as if he anticipated the entire exercise if he does. Be sure to say his name the same way you would if you were going to follow it with a recall command.
   C. Leave the dog and run to the opposite side of the room.
5) A. Do the same thing as in answer # 4. Put a long line on the dog and cause him to resist the tension on the line.
   B. Have a person come up from behind and gently nudge the dog to move.
6) A. Send the dog on a go-out and intentionally stop him very short (just at the jumps or before) three times in a row. Then send him and see if he stops on his own. If he does, you are in a position to show him his mistake.
   B. Put the dog on a Flexi-lead or long-line and make the dog do a full distance go-out pulling the line out away from you. There should be slight tension on the line.
   C. Set up a Utility ring that is half on concrete and half on grass. Do not worry if there is a curb at the end of the concrete. Send the dog on a Go-Out. He is likely to stop short at the end of the concrete and not venture onto the grass. When he does, you are in a position to show him his mistake.

Answers...cont'.

Page 66
1. c   2. a, b & c   3. a, b, c & d   4. b   5. a

Page 67
Case # 1

Midnight is afraid of the judge who is standing and/or walking behind her as she starts her recall. Being small, she fears being stepped on if she suddenly drops, especially when she hears footsteps behind her.

Realizing this, the trainer proofs Midnight with a person walking behind. At first Midnight doesn't drop (like in the trial) but after being made to drop by her trainer who gently pushes her to the floor, Midnight begins to trust. Th proof is continued until Midnight will drop and allow the acting judge to slowly step over her. Midnight's fears have been resolved and guess what, in the next shows she does a drop on recall everytime!

Page 68
Case # 2

When the handler is closer to the boards the dog knows the handler's foot could reach him. The key is to have a correction occur while the handler is 2' away. The solution is to have the handler in practi stand 2' away and have an "arm extender" such as a dowel in her hand.

That way, if the dog tries to land near the corner, the "arm extender" can reach out and bump the dog, the same way as the leg had. Now the dog knows a correction can occur at 2' away!

Page 69
Case # 3

The dog thinks that she is at a Go–Out. She expects a jump signal. The dog doesn't know she can do a recall in between the jumps. The handler helps the dog by going to her and gently bringing the dog through the jump as she praises. The next time the dog was set up to do a recall the dog flew in to her handler, knowing it that was okay to come in between the jumps.

ANSWERS

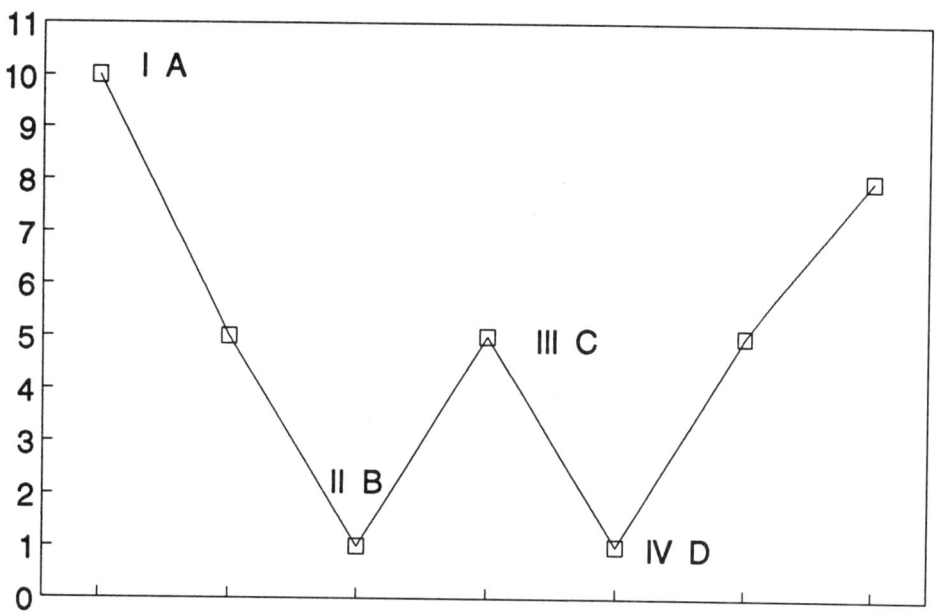

Pages 95 – 96

ANSWERS:

In the Novice Ring:

1) F
2) T
3) F
4) F
5) F
6) T
7) T
8) F
9) T
10) T

In the Open Ring:

1) F
2) F
3) T
4) F
5) F
6) F
7) T
8) F
9) F
10) F

In the Utility Ring:

1) F
2) F
3) F
4) T
5) T
6) F
7) F
8) T
9) F
10) T
11) F
12) T – A poor pivot can be considered an aid to the dog.
13) T – The judge wants to see that you stopped the dog, not the gate.

If you are confused about any of these answers search for the explanation in your AKC – Obedience Rule Book.

You do have one.... Don't you!

ANSWERS PAGE 97 – 98

A   1) Standards for bar jump are not white.
     2) High jump is not white.
     3) Armband should be on your left arm.
     4) Poodle cannot have a *fancy* bow in her hair.
     5) Dog wearing a spiked collar.
     6) Dog off leash with its handler outside the ring.
     7) Car parked closer than 50' to the ring.
     8) Judge sitting in one place so he cannot be in position to see the dog.
     9) Double handling with a person outside the ring.

B   1) Wearing a shirt to show a dog makes it difficult for the dog to see heel position.
     2) Cats at dog shows are rarely welcomed.
     3) Food on the judges table doesn't help your dog pay attention to you.
     4) Nasty dogs and commotion outside the ring.
     5) Stray dogs running through the ring.

ANSWERS: Page 102/103 – JUMPING JUMBLE
Regarding Jumping ……………

Use a <u>RENTFIFED</u> verbal command for each jump, in direct jumping.

<u>D</u> <u>I</u> <u>F</u> <u>F</u> <u>E</u> <u>R</u> <u>E</u> <u>N</u> <u>T</u>

On retrieve over the high jump, teach the <u>TRERUN</u> before you ever throw a dumbbell over the jump.

<u>R</u> <u>E</u> <u>T</u> <u>U</u> <u>R</u> <u>N</u>

When giving a directed jumping signal, show the dog your <u>LAMP</u> before lifting the hand signal.

<u>P</u> <u>A</u> <u>L</u> <u>M</u>

If the dog takes the <u>GROWN</u> jump, continue to hold the signal, until the dog knows he's made a mistake, then walk back and start again.

<u>W</u> <u>R</u> <u>O</u> <u>N</u> <u>G</u>

Jumping Answers..Cont'.

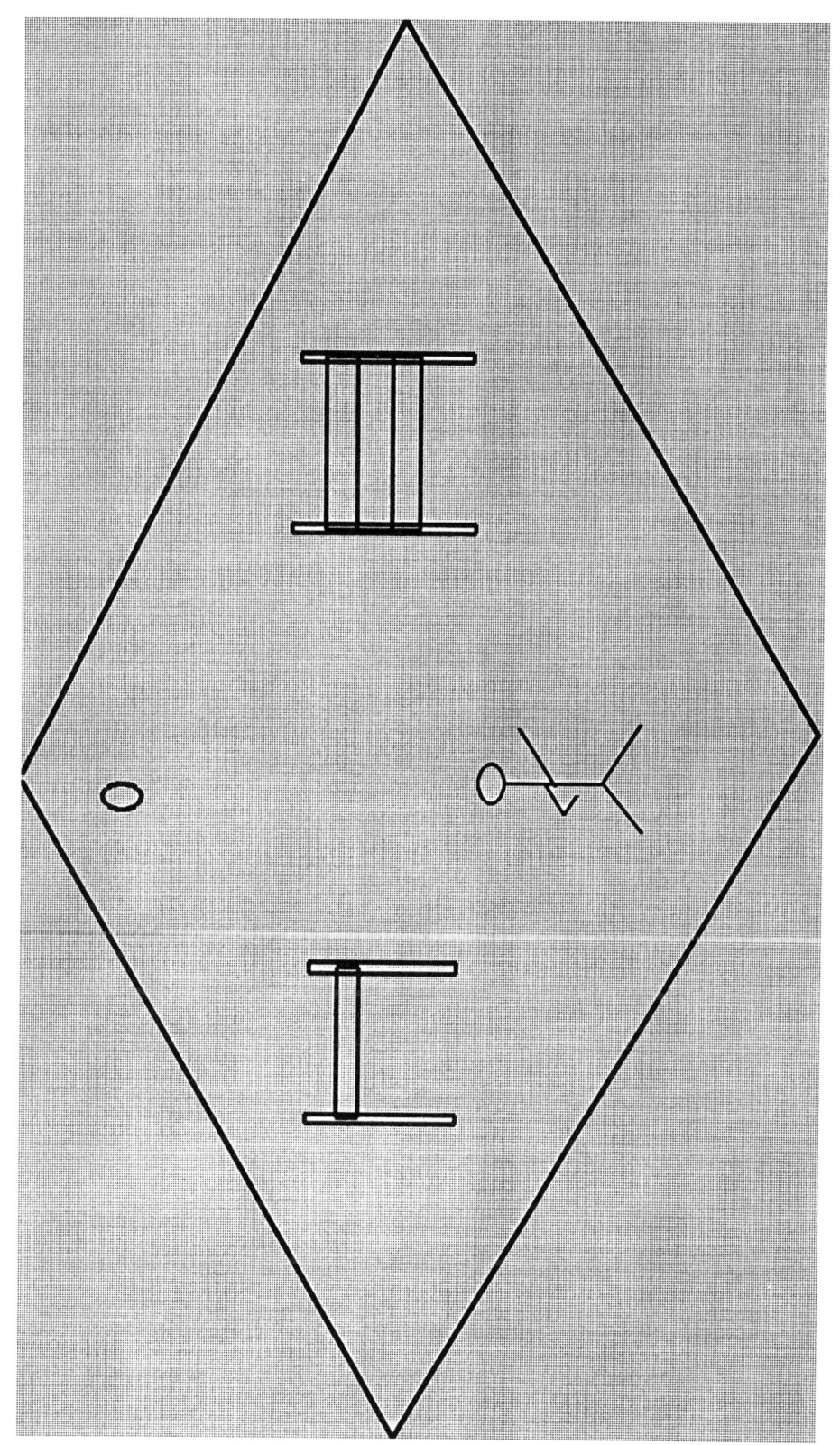

The Utility ring is diamond shaped, so when giving the signal, position your arm FORWARD of your body.

Answers...cont'

Page 104 – 109

Scene One:
D

Although B is a "help" answer, the reasoning is incorrect. C and A are also incorrect because there is no reason to pinch this dog.

Scene Two:
B

Letter D is incorrect because we know the dog IS afraid
(re-read the description of her posture.)

Scene Three:
D

Pinching is the answer to this scene, but letter B is not correct, even though it is a pinch solution. The reasoning of B is the dog should have been pinched right away, and she was right in waiting until the next time.

Scene Four:
B

There is no problem with the dog's ability to retrieve as suggested in letter C, and if she waits any longer (as suggested in letter A), the dog will continue in this pattern, which seems to have become comfortable for him. Letter D is clearly untrue as we know the dog is diligently working the pile, and Bichons, like all breeds, certainly can and do show stress.

Answers...Cont'.
OBEDIENCE CROSSWORD PUZZLE – ANSWERS page 110/111

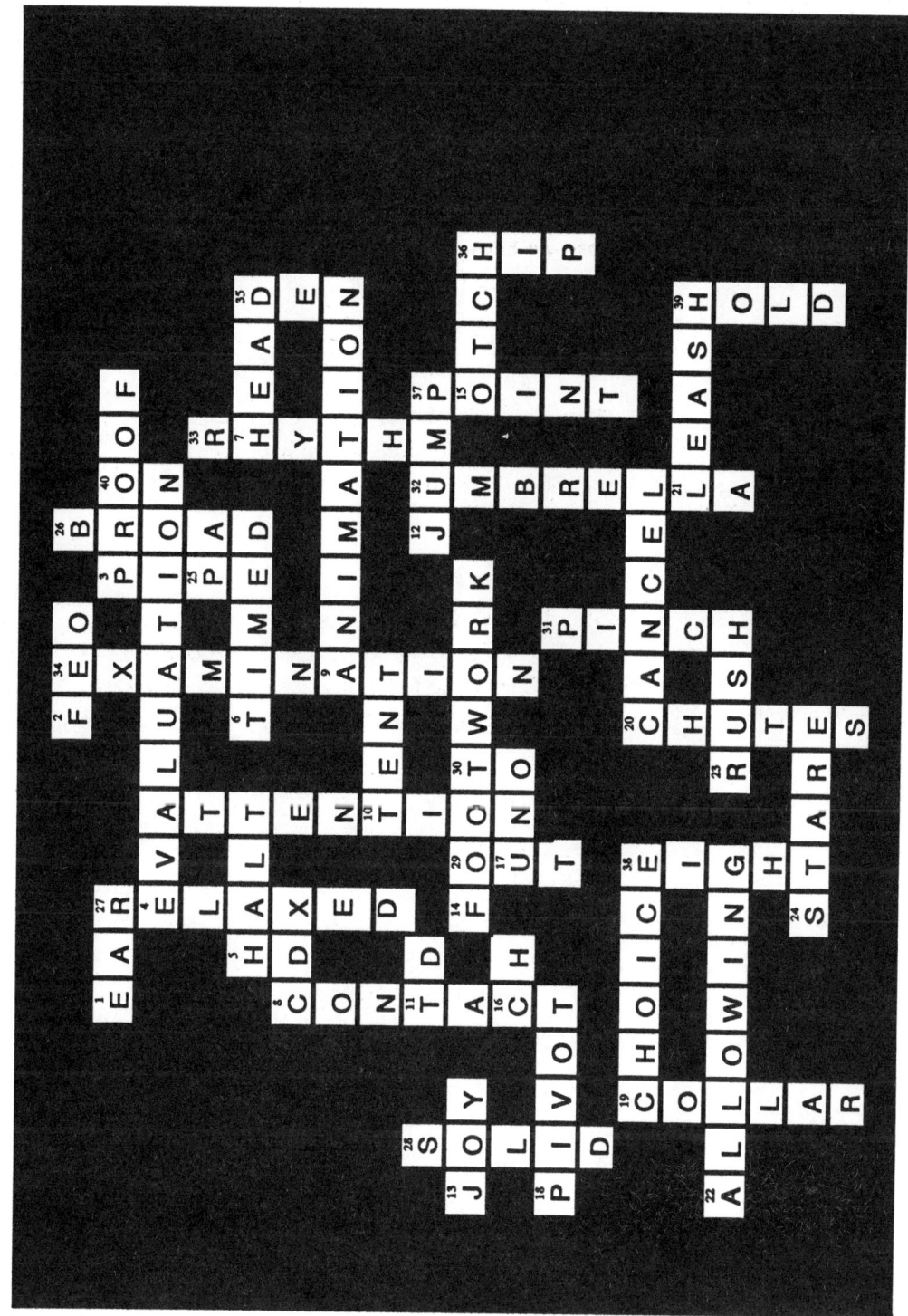

173

NOTES

NOTES

NOTES

NOTES

NOTES

NOTES

NOTES

MATCH SHOW - LOG

Name of Match/Show: _____   Date: _____
Location (I/O): _____   Weather: _____
Ring Conditions: _____   Judge: _____
Class: _____   Your Goal: _____
Did you accomplish your goal?: _____

Things dog did well: _____

What things distracted your dog that surprised you?: _____

What proofs do you plan to do?: _____

Not Perfect Yet: _____

Score (if any): ☐   Score Breakdown

Leg or Title?: ☐

★ Why did the dog lose points?
★ Did you notice your need for more proofing?
★ Did you correct at a Match
★ Were there unusual conditions?

Exercise	Max Score	Your Score	Comments
TOTAL:			

Was this the dog's first, second, third, etc...class of the day?: _____

What did you learn from this experience?: _____

(circle all that apply)

HOW DID YOU FEEL IN THE RING?   Rhythmical

    In Control   Forgot Footwork

    Nervous   Did more than my job

    Excited   Out of Rhythm

    Relaxed   Moved too slow

    Focused   Moved too fast

MATCH SHOW - LOG

Name of Match/Show: _____ Date: _____
Location (I/O): _____ Weather: _____
Ring Conditions: _____ Judge: _____
Class: _____ Your Goal: _____
Did you accomplish your goal?: _____
_____

Things dog did well: _____
_____

What things distracted your dog
that surprised you?: _____
_____

What proofs do you plan to do?: _____
_____

Not Perfect Yet: _____

Score (if any): [   ]   Score Breakdown

Leg or Title?: [   ]

🔸 Why did the dog lose points?
🔸 Did you notice your need for more proofing?
🔸 Did you correct at a Match
🔸 Were there unusual conditions?

Exercise	Max Score	Your Score	Comments
TOTAL:			

Was this the dog's first, second,
third, etc...class of the day?: _____

What did you learn from this
experience?: _____

(circle all that apply)

HOW DID YOU FEEL IN THE RING?   Rhythmical

                In Control   Forgot Footwork

                Nervous   Did more than my job

                Excited   Out of Rhythm

                Relaxed   Moved too slow

                Focused   Moved too fast

MATCH SHOW - LOG

Name of Match/Show: _____ Date: _____
Location (I/O): _____ Weather: _____
Ring Conditions: _____ Judge: _____
Class: _____ Your Goal: _____
Did you accomplish your goal?: _____

Things dog did well: _____

What things distracted your dog that surprised you?: _____

What proofs do you plan to do?: _____

Not Perfect Yet: _____

Score (if any): [   ]

Leg or Title?: [   ]

Score Breakdown

♣ Why did the dog lose points?
♣ Did you notice your need for more proofing?
♣ Did you correct at a Match
♣ Were there unusual conditions?

Exercise	Max Score	Your Score	Comments
TOTAL:			

Was this the dog's first, second, third, etc...class of the day?: _____

What did you learn from this experience?: _____

(circle all that apply)

HOW DID YOU FEEL IN THE RING?

Rhythmical

In Control   Forgot Footwork

Nervous   Did more than my job

Excited   Out of Rhythm

Relaxed   Moved too slow

Focused   Moved too fast

MATCH SHOW - LOG

Name of Match/Show: _____   Date: _____
Location (I/O): _____   Weather: _____
Ring Conditions: _____   Judge: _____
Class: _____   Your Goal: _____
Did you accomplish your goal?: _____
_____

Things dog did well: _____
_____

What things distracted your dog
that surprised you?: _____
_____

What proofs do you plan to do?: _____
_____

Not Perfect Yet: _____

Score (if any): [_____]

Score Breakdown

♣ Why did the dog lose points?
♣ Did you notice your need for more proofing?
♣ Did you correct at a Match
♣ Were there unusual conditions?

Leg or Title?: [_____]

Exercise	Max Score	Your Score	Comments
TOTAL:			

Was this the dog's first, second,
third, etc...class of the day?: _____

What did you learn from this
experience?: _____

(circle all that apply)

HOW DID YOU FEEL IN THE RING?   Rhythmical

           In Control   Forgot Footwork

           Nervous   Did more than my job

           Excited   Out of Rhythm

           Relaxed   Moved too slow

           Focused   Moved too fast

MATCH SHOW - LOG

Name of Match/Show: _____ Date: _____
Location (I/O): _____ Weather: _____
Ring Conditions: _____ Judge: _____
Class: _____ Your Goal: _____
Did you accomplish your goal?: _____

Things dog did well: _____

What things distracted your dog
that surprised you?: _____

What proofs do you plan to do?: _____

Not Perfect Yet: _____

Score (if any): [   ]
                                    Score Breakdown
Leg or Title?: [   ]

♣ Why did the dog lose points?
♣ Did you notice your need for more proofing?
♣ Did you correct at a Match
♣ Were there unusual conditions?

Exercise	Max Score	Your Score	Comments
TOTAL:			

Was this the dog's first, second,
third, etc...class of the day?: _____

What did you learn from this
experience?: _____

(circle all that apply)

HOW DID YOU FEEL IN THE RING?   Rhythmical

                    In Control   Forgot Footwork

                    Nervous   Did more than my job

                    Excited   Out of Rhythm

                    Relaxed   Moved too slow

                    Focused   Moved too fast

MATCH SHOW - LOG

Name of Match/Show: _____   Date: _____
Location (I/O): _____   Weather: _____
Ring Conditions: _____   Judge: _____
Class: _____   Your Goal: _____
Did you accomplish your goal?: _____
_____
Things dog did well: _____
_____
What things distracted your dog
that surprised you?: _____
_____
What proofs do you plan to do?: _____
_____
Not Perfect Yet: _____

Score (if any): [   ]   Score Breakdown   ❧ Why did the dog lose points?
                                                    ❧ Did you notice your need for more proofing?
Leg or Title?: [   ]   ❧ Did you correct at a Match
                                                    ❧ Were there unusual conditions?

Exercise	Max Score	Your Score	Comments
TOTAL:			

Was this the dog's first, second,
third, etc...class of the day?: _____

What did you learn from this
experience?: _____

(circle all that apply)

HOW DID YOU FEEL IN THE RING?   Rhythmical

                    In Control   Forgot Footwork

                    Nervous   Did more than my job

                    Excited   Out of Rhythm

                    Relaxed   Moved too slow

                    Focused   Moved too fast

MATCH SHOW - LOG

Name of Match/Show: _____ Date: _____

Location (I/O): _____ Weather: _____

Ring Conditions: _____ Judge: _____

Class: _____ Your Goal: _____

Did you accomplish your goal?: _____

Things dog did well: _____

What things distracted your dog that surprised you?: _____

What proofs do you plan to do?: _____

Not Perfect Yet: _____

Score (if any): [____]

Leg or Title?: [____]

Score Breakdown

♣ Why did the dog lose points?
♣ Did you notice your need for more proofing?
♣ Did you correct at a Match
♣ Were there unusual conditions?

Exercise	Max Score	Your Score	Comments
TOTAL:			

Was this the dog's first, second, third, etc...class of the day?: _____

What did you learn from this experience?: _____

(circle all that apply)

HOW DID YOU FEEL IN THE RING?   Rhythmical

                    In Control   Forgot Footwork

                    Nervous   Did more than my job

                    Excited   Out of Rhythm

                    Relaxed   Moved too slow

                    Focused   Moved too fast

MATCH SHOW - LOG

Name of Match/Show: _____   Date: _____
Location (I/O): _____   Weather: _____
Ring Conditions: _____   Judge: _____
Class: _____   Your Goal: _____
Did you accomplish your goal?: _____

Things dog did well: _____

What things distracted your dog
that surprised you?: _____

What proofs do you plan to do?: _____

Not Perfect Yet: _____

Score (if any): [   ]   Score Breakdown   ♣ Why did the dog lose points?
                                                           ♣ Did you notice your need for more proofing?
Leg or Title?: [   ]   ♣ Did you correct at a Match
                                                           ♣ Were there unusual conditions?

Exercise	Max Score	Your Score	Comments
TOTAL:			

Was this the dog's first, second,
third, etc...class of the day?: _____

What did you learn from this
experience?: _____

(circle all that apply)

HOW DID YOU FEEL IN THE RING?   Rhythmical

                        In Control   Forgot Footwork

                        Nervous   Did more than my job

                        Excited   Out of Rhythm

                        Relaxed   Moved too slow

                        Focused   Moved too fast

MATCH SHOW - LOG

Name of Match/Show: _____ Date: _____
Location (I/O): _____ Weather: _____
Ring Conditions: _____ Judge: _____
Class: _____ Your Goal: _____
Did you accomplish your goal?: _____
_____

Things dog did well: _____
_____

What things distracted your dog
that surprised you?: _____
_____

What proofs do you plan to do?: _____
_____

Not Perfect Yet: _____

Score (if any): ☐
⠀⠀⠀⠀⠀⠀⠀⠀⠀⠀⠀⠀Score Breakdown

✱ Why did the dog lose points?
✱ Did you notice your need for more proofing?
✱ Did you correct at a Match
✱ Were there unusual conditions?

Leg or Title?: ☐

Exercise	Max Score	Your Score	Comments
TOTAL:			

Was this the dog's first, second,
third, etc...class of the day?: _____

What did you learn from this
experience?: _____

(circle all that apply)

HOW DID YOU FEEL IN THE RING?⠀⠀⠀⠀⠀Rhythmical

⠀⠀⠀⠀⠀⠀⠀⠀⠀⠀⠀⠀⠀⠀⠀⠀⠀⠀In Control⠀⠀Forgot Footwork

⠀⠀⠀⠀⠀⠀⠀⠀⠀⠀⠀⠀⠀⠀⠀⠀⠀⠀Nervous⠀⠀Did more than my job

⠀⠀⠀⠀⠀⠀⠀⠀⠀⠀⠀⠀⠀⠀⠀⠀⠀⠀Excited⠀⠀Out of Rhythm

⠀⠀⠀⠀⠀⠀⠀⠀⠀⠀⠀⠀⠀⠀⠀⠀⠀⠀Relaxed⠀⠀Moved too slow

⠀⠀⠀⠀⠀⠀⠀⠀⠀⠀⠀⠀⠀⠀⠀⠀⠀⠀Focused⠀⠀Moved too fast

MATCH SHOW - LOG

Name of Match/Show: _____ Date: _____
Location (I/O): _____ Weather: _____
Ring Conditions: _____ Judge: _____
Class: _____ Your Goal: _____

Did you accomplish your goal?: _____
_____

Things dog did well: _____
_____

What things distracted your dog
that surprised you?: _____
_____

What proofs do you plan to do?: _____
_____

Not Perfect Yet: _____

Score (if any): [   ]

Score Breakdown

♣ Why did the dog lose points?
♣ Did you notice your need for more proofing?

Leg or Title?: [   ]

♣ Did you correct at a Match
♣ Were there unusual conditions?

Exercise	Max Score	Your Score	Comments
TOTAL:			

Was this the dog's first, second,
third, etc...class of the day?: _____

What did you learn from this
experience?: _____

(circle all that apply)

HOW DID YOU FEEL IN THE RING?   Rhythmical

                        In Control   Forgot Footwork

                        Nervous   Did more than my job

                        Excited   Out of Rhythm

                        Relaxed   Moved too slow

                        Focused   Moved too fast

MATCH SHOW - LOG

Name of Match/Show: _____ Date: _____
Location (I/O): _____ Weather: _____
Ring Conditions: _____ Judge: _____
Class: _____ Your Goal: _____

Did you accomplish your goal?: _____

Things dog did well: _____

What things distracted your dog that surprised you?: _____

What proofs do you plan to do?: _____

Not Perfect Yet: _____

Score (if any): [   ]

Score Breakdown

♣ Why did the dog lose points?
♣ Did you notice your need for more proofing?
♣ Did you correct at a Match
♣ Were there unusual conditions?

Leg or Title?: [   ]

Exercise	Max Score	Your Score	Comments
TOTAL:			

Was this the dog's first, second, third, etc...class of the day?: _____

What did you learn from this experience?: _____

(circle all that apply)

HOW DID YOU FEEL IN THE RING?   Rhythmical

In Control   Forgot Footwork

Nervous   Did more than my job

Excited   Out of Rhythm

Relaxed   Moved too slow

Focused   Moved too fast

MATCH SHOW - LOG

Name of Match/Show: _____ Date: _____
Location (I/O): _____ Weather: _____
Ring Conditions: _____ Judge: _____
Class: _____ Your Goal: _____

Did you accomplish your goal?: _____
_____

Things dog did well: _____
_____

What things distracted your dog
that surprised you?: _____
_____

What proofs do you plan to do?: _____
_____

Not Perfect Yet: _____

Score (if any): [_____]

Score Breakdown

🌿 Why did the dog lose points?
🌿 Did you notice your need for more proofing?
🌿 Did you correct at a Match
🌿 Were there unusual conditions?

Leg or Title?: [_____]

Exercise	Max Score	Your Score	Comments
TOTAL:			

Was this the dog's first, second,
third, etc...class of the day?: _____

What did you learn from this
experience?: _____

(circle all that apply)

HOW DID YOU FEEL IN THE RING?   Rhythmical

         In Control Forgot Footwork

         Nervous Did more than my job

         Excited Out of Rhythm

         Relaxed Moved too slow

         Focused Moved too fast

MATCH SHOW - LOG

Name of Match/Show: _____   Date: _____
Location (I/O): _____   Weather: _____
Ring Conditions: _____   Judge: _____
Class: _____   Your Goal: _____
Did you accomplish your goal?: _____
_____

Things dog did well: _____
_____

What things distracted your dog
that surprised you?: _____
_____

What proofs do you plan to do?: _____
_____

Not Perfect Yet: _____

Score (if any): [_____]

Score Breakdown

- Why did the dog lose points?
- Did you notice your need for more proofing?
- Did you correct at a Match
- Were there unusual conditions?

Leg or Title?: [_____]

Exercise	Max Score	Your Score	Comments
TOTAL:			

Was this the dog's first, second,
third, etc...class of the day?: _____

What did you learn from this _____
experience?: _____

(circle all that apply)

HOW DID YOU FEEL IN THE RING?   Rhythmical

        In Control   Forgot Footwork

        Nervous   Did more than my job

        Excited   Out of Rhythm

        Relaxed   Moved too slow

        Focused   Moved too fast

MATCH SHOW - LOG

Name of Match/Show: _____ Date: _____
Location (I/O): _____ Weather: _____
Ring Conditions: _____ Judge: _____
Class: _____ Your Goal: _____
Did you accomplish your goal?: _____
_____
Things dog did well: _____
_____
What things distracted your dog
that surprised you?: _____
_____
What proofs do you plan to do?: _____
_____
Not Perfect Yet: _____

Score (if any): [____]

Score Breakdown

♣ Why did the dog lose points?
♣ Did you notice your need for more proofing?
♣ Did you correct at a Match
♣ Were there unusual conditions?

Leg or Title?: [____]

Exercise	Max Score	Your Score	Comments
TOTAL:			

Was this the dog's first, second,
third, etc...class of the day?: _____

What did you learn from this
experience?: _____

(circle all that apply)

HOW DID YOU FEEL IN THE RING?   Rhythmical

                In Control   Forgot Footwork

                Nervous   Did more than my job

                Excited   Out of Rhythm

                Relaxed   Moved too slow

                Focused   Moved too fast

MATCH SHOW - LOG

Name of Match/Show: _____   Date: _____
Location (I/O): _____   Weather: _____
Ring Conditions: _____   Judge: _____
Class: _____   Your Goal: _____
Did you accomplish your goal?: _____

Things dog did well: _____

What things distracted your dog
that surprised you?: _____

What proofs do you plan to do?: _____

Not Perfect Yet: _____

Score (if any): [_____]

Score Breakdown

- Why did the dog lose points?
- Did you notice your need for more proofing?
- Did you correct at a Match
- Were there unusual conditions?

Leg or Title?: [_____]

Exercise	Max Score	Your Score	Comments
TOTAL:			

Was this the dog's first, second,
third, etc...class of the day?: _____

What did you learn from this
experience?: _____

(circle all that apply)

HOW DID YOU FEEL IN THE RING?   Rhythmical

                    In Control   Forgot Footwork

                    Nervous   Did more than my job

                    Excited   Out of Rhythm

                    Relaxed   Moved too slow

                    Focused   Moved too fast

MATCH SHOW - LOG

Name of Match/Show: _____   Date: _____
Location (I/O): _____   Weather: _____
Ring Conditions: _____   Judge: _____
Class: _____   Your Goal: _____

Did you accomplish your goal?: _____

Things dog did well: _____

What things distracted your dog
that surprised you?: _____

What proofs do you plan to do?: _____

Not Perfect Yet: _____

Score (if any): [   ]

Score Breakdown

♣ Why did the dog lose points?
♣ Did you notice your need for more proofing?
♣ Did you correct at a Match
♣ Were there unusual conditions?

Leg or Title?: [   ]

Exercise	Max Score	Your Score	Comments
TOTAL:			

Was this the dog's first, second,
third, etc...class of the day?: _____

What did you learn from this
experience?: _____

(circle all that apply)

HOW DID YOU FEEL IN THE RING?

Rhythmical

In Control   Forgot Footwork

Nervous   Did more than my job

Excited   Out of Rhythm

Relaxed   Moved too slow

Focused   Moved too fast

MATCH SHOW - LOG

Name of Match/Show: _____   Date: _____
Location (I/O): _____   Weather: _____
Ring Conditions: _____   Judge: _____
Class: _____   Your Goal: _____

Did you accomplish your goal?: _____
_____

Things dog did well: _____
_____

What things distracted your dog
that surprised you?: _____
_____

What proofs do you plan to do?: _____
_____

Not Perfect Yet: _____

Score (if any): [_____]   Score Breakdown

Leg or Title?: [_____]

✦ Why did the dog lose points?
✦ Did you notice your need for more proofing?
✦ Did you correct at a Match
✦ Were there unusual conditions?

Exercise	Max Score	Your Score	Comments
TOTAL:			

Was this the dog's first, second,
third, etc...class of the day?: _____

What did you learn from this
experience?: _____

(circle all that apply)

HOW DID YOU FEEL IN THE RING?   Rhythmical

        In Control   Forgot Footwork

        Nervous   Did more than my job

        Excited   Out of Rhythm

        Relaxed   Moved too slow

        Focused   Moved too fast

MATCH SHOW – LOG

Name of Match/Show: _____   Date: _____
Location (I/O): _____   Weather: _____
Ring Conditions: _____   Judge: _____
Class: _____   Your Goal: _____
Did you accomplish your goal?: _____
_____

Things dog did well: _____
_____

What things distracted your dog
that surprised you?: _____
_____

What proofs do you plan to do?: _____
_____

Not Perfect Yet: _____

Score (if any): [_____]   Score Breakdown
- Why did the dog lose points?
- Did you notice your need for more proofing?
Leg or Title?: [_____]
- Did you correct at a Match
- Were there unusual conditions?

Exercise	Max Score	Your Score	Comments
TOTAL:			

Was this the dog's first, second,
third, etc...class of the day?: _____

What did you learn from this
experience?: _____

(circle all that apply)

HOW DID YOU FEEL IN THE RING?   Rhythmical

    In Control   Forgot Footwork

    Nervous   Did more than my job

    Excited   Out of Rhythm

    Relaxed   Moved too slow

    Focused   Moved too fast

MATCH SHOW - LOG

Name of Match/Show: _____ Date: _____
Location (I/O): _____ Weather: _____
Ring Conditions: _____ Judge: _____
Class: _____ Your Goal: _____
Did you accomplish your goal?: _____

Things dog did well: _____

What things distracted your dog that surprised you?: _____

What proofs do you plan to do?: _____

Not Perfect Yet: _____

Score (if any): [   ]

Score Breakdown

- Why did the dog lose points?
- Did you notice your need for more proofing?
- Did you correct at a Match
- Were there unusual conditions?

Leg or Title?: [   ]

Exercise	Max Score	Your Score	Comments
TOTAL:			

Was this the dog's first, second, third, etc...class of the day?: _____

What did you learn from this experience?: _____

(circle all that apply)

HOW DID YOU FEEL IN THE RING?   Rhythmical

                        In Control   Forgot Footwork

                        Nervous   Did more than my job

                        Excited   Out of Rhythm

                        Relaxed   Moved too slow

                        Focused   Moved too fast

MATCH SHOW - LOG

Name of Match/Show: _____ Date: _____
Location (I/O): _____ Weather: _____
Ring Conditions: _____ Judge: _____
Class: _____ Your Goal: _____

Did you accomplish your goal?: _____
_____

Things dog did well: _____
_____

What things distracted your dog
that surprised you?: _____
_____

What proofs do you plan to do?: _____
_____

Not Perfect Yet: _____

Score (if any): [   ]

Score Breakdown

♣ Why did the dog lose points?
♣ Did you notice your need for more proofing?
♣ Did you correct at a Match
♣ Were there unusual conditions?

Leg or Title?: [   ]

Exercise	Max Score	Your Score	Comments
TOTAL:			

Was this the dog's first, second,
third, etc...class of the day?: _____

What did you learn from this _____
experience?: _____

(circle all that apply)

HOW DID YOU FEEL IN THE RING?   Rhythmical

                                          In Control   Forgot Footwork

                                          Nervous   Did more than my job

                                          Excited   Out of Rhythm

                                          Relaxed   Moved too slow

                                          Focused   Moved too fast

MATCH SHOW - LOG

Name of Match/Show: _____   Date: _____
Location (I/O): _____   Weather: _____
Ring Conditions: _____   Judge: _____
Class: _____   Your Goal: _____
Did you accomplish your goal?: _____
_____

Things dog did well: _____
_____

What things distracted your dog
that surprised you?: _____
_____

What proofs do you plan to do?: _____
_____

Not Perfect Yet: _____

Score (if any): [____]

Score Breakdown

♣ Why did the dog lose points?
♣ Did you notice your need for more proofing?
♣ Did you correct at a Match
♣ Were there unusual conditions?

Leg or Title?: [____]

Exercise	Max Score	Your Score	Comments
TOTAL:			

Was this the dog's first, second,
third, etc...class of the day?: _____

What did you learn from this
experience?: _____

(circle all that apply)

HOW DID YOU FEEL IN THE RING?   Rhythmical

        In Control   Forgot Footwork

        Nervous   Did more than my job

        Excited   Out of Rhythm

        Relaxed   Moved too slow

        Focused   Moved too fast

MATCH SHOW - LOG

Name of Match/Show: _____   Date: _____
Location (I/O): _____   Weather: _____
Ring Conditions: _____   Judge: _____
Class: _____   Your Goal: _____

Did you accomplish your goal?: _____
_____

Things dog did well: _____
_____

What things distracted your dog
that surprised you?: _____
_____

What proofs do you plan to do?: _____
_____

Not Perfect Yet: _____

Score (if any): [   ]   Score Breakdown

Leg or Title?: [   ]

- Why did the dog lose points?
- Did you notice your need for more proofing?
- Did you correct at a Match
- Were there unusual conditions?

Exercise	Max Score	Your Score	Comments
TOTAL:			

Was this the dog's first, second,
third, etc...class of the day?: _____

What did you learn from this
experience?: _____

(circle all that apply)

HOW DID YOU FEEL IN THE RING?   Rhythmical

                                            In Control   Forgot Footwork

                                            Nervous   Did more than my job

                                            Excited   Out of Rhythm

                                            Relaxed   Moved too slow

                                            Focused   Moved too fast

MATCH SHOW - LOG

Name of Match/Show: _____ Date: _____
Location (I/O): _____ Weather: _____
Ring Conditions: _____ Judge: _____
Class: _____ Your Goal: _____
Did you accomplish your goal?: _____

Things dog did well: _____

What things distracted your dog
that surprised you?: _____

What proofs do you plan to do?: _____

Not Perfect Yet: _____

Score (if any): [____]   **Score Breakdown**   ♦ Why did the dog lose points?
                                                              ♦ Did you notice your need for more proofing?
Leg or Title?: [____]   ♦ Did you correct at a Match
                                                              ♦ Were there unusual conditions?

Exercise	Max Score	Your Score	Comments
TOTAL:			

Was this the dog's first, second,
third, etc...class of the day?: _____

What did you learn from this
experience?: _____

(circle all that apply)

HOW DID YOU FEEL IN THE RING?   Rhythmical

                    In Control   Forgot Footwork

                    Nervous   Did more than my job

                    Excited   Out of Rhythm

                    Relaxed   Moved too slow

                    Focused   Moved too fast

MATCH SHOW - LOG

Name of Match/Show: _____ Date: _____

Location (I/O): _____ Weather: _____

Ring Conditions: _____ Judge: _____

Class: _____ Your Goal: _____

Did you accomplish your goal?: _____

Things dog did well: _____

What things distracted your dog that surprised you?: _____

What proofs do you plan to do?: _____

Not Perfect Yet: _____

Score (if any): [____]

Leg or Title?: [____]

Score Breakdown

- Why did the dog lose points?
- Did you notice your need for more proofing?
- Did you correct at a Match
- Were there unusual conditions?

Exercise	Max Score	Your Score	Comments
TOTAL:			

Was this the dog's first, second, third, etc...class of the day?: _____

What did you learn from this experience?: _____

(circle all that apply)

HOW DID YOU FEEL IN THE RING?   Rhythmical

    In Control   Forgot Footwork

    Nervous   Did more than my job

    Excited   Out of Rhythm

    Relaxed   Moved too slow

    Focused   Moved too fast

MATCH SHOW - LOG

Name of Match/Show: _____ Date: _____
Location (I/O): _____ Weather: _____
Ring Conditions: _____ Judge: _____
Class: _____ Your Goal: _____
Did you accomplish your goal?: _____
_____
Things dog did well: _____
_____
What things distracted your dog
that surprised you?: _____
_____
What proofs do you plan to do?: _____
_____
Not Perfect Yet: _____

Score (if any): [   ]

Score Breakdown

♣ Why did the dog lose points?
♣ Did you notice your need for more proofing?
♣ Did you correct at a Match
♣ Were there unusual conditions?

Leg or Title?: [   ]

Exercise	Max Score	Your Score	Comments
TOTAL:			

Was this the dog's first, second,
third, etc...class of the day?: _____

What did you learn from this
experience?: _____

(circle all that apply)

HOW DID YOU FEEL IN THE RING?   Rhythmical

        In Control   Forgot Footwork

        Nervous   Did more than my job

        Excited   Out of Rhythm

        Relaxed   Moved too slow

        Focused   Moved too fast

MATCH SHOW - LOG

Name of Match/Show: _____ Date: _____
Location (I/O): _____ Weather: _____
Ring Conditions: _____ Judge: _____
Class: _____ Your Goal: _____

Did you accomplish your goal?: _____
_____

Things dog did well: _____
_____

What things distracted your dog
that surprised you?: _____
_____

What proofs do you plan to do?: _____
_____

Not Perfect Yet: _____

Score (if any): [_____]

          Score Breakdown

- Why did the dog lose points?
- Did you notice your need for more proofing?
- Did you correct at a Match
- Were there unusual conditions?

Leg or Title?: [_____]

Exercise	Max Score	Your Score	Comments
TOTAL:			

Was this the dog's first, second,
third, etc...class of the day?: _____

What did you learn from this
experience?: _____

(circle all that apply)

HOW DID YOU FEEL IN THE RING?   Rhythmical

                                     In Control   Forgot Footwork

                                     Nervous   Did more than my job

                                       Excited   Out of Rhythm

                                       Relaxed   Moved too slow

                                       Focused   Moved too fast

MATCH SHOW - LOG

Name of Match/Show: _____ Date: _____
Location (I/O): _____ Weather: _____
Ring Conditions: _____ Judge: _____
Class: _____ Your Goal: _____
Did you accomplish your goal?: _____
_____

Things dog did well: _____
_____

What things distracted your dog
that surprised you?: _____
_____

What proofs do you plan to do?: _____
_____

Not Perfect Yet: _____
_____

Score (if any): [   ]

Score Breakdown

- Why did the dog lose points?
- Did you notice your need for more proofing?
- Did you correct at a Match
- Were there unusual conditions?

Leg or Title?: [   ]

Exercise	Max Score	Your Score	Comments
TOTAL:			

Was this the dog's first, second,
third, etc...class of the day?: _____

What did you learn from this
experience?: _____
_____

(circle all that apply)

HOW DID YOU FEEL IN THE RING?   Rhythmical

                In Control   Forgot Footwork

                Nervous   Did more than my job

                Excited   Out of Rhythm

                Relaxed   Moved too slow

                Focused   Moved too fast

MATCH SHOW - LOG

Name of Match/Show: _____ Date: _____
Location (I/O): _____ Weather: _____
Ring Conditions: _____ Judge: _____
Class: _____ Your Goal: _____
Did you accomplish your goal?: _____
_____
Things dog did well: _____
_____
What things distracted your dog
that surprised you?: _____
_____
What proofs do you plan to do?: _____
_____
Not Perfect Yet: _____

Score (if any): [_____]   Score Breakdown   ♣ Why did the dog lose points?
                                               ♣ Did you notice your need for more proofing?
Leg or Title?: [_____]   ♣ Did you correct at a Match
                                               ♣ Were there unusual conditions?

Exercise	Max Score	Your Score	Comments
TOTAL:			

Was this the dog's first, second,
third, etc...class of the day?: _____

What did you learn from this _____
experience?: _____

(circle all that apply)

HOW DID YOU FEEL IN THE RING?   Rhythmical

                    In Control   Forgot Footwork

                    Nervous   Did more than my job

                    Excited   Out of Rhythm

                    Relaxed   Moved too slow

                    Focused   Moved too fast

MATCH SHOW - LOG

Name of Match/Show: _____   Date: _____
Location (I/O): _____   Weather: _____
Ring Conditions: _____   Judge: _____
Class: _____   Your Goal: _____
Did you accomplish your goal?: _____
_____
Things dog did well: _____
_____
What things distracted your dog
that surprised you?: _____
_____
What proofs do you plan to do?: _____
_____
Not Perfect Yet: _____

Score (if any): [_____]

Leg or Title?: [_____]

Score Breakdown

★ Why did the dog lose points?
★ Did you notice your need for more proofing?
★ Did you correct at a Match
★ Were there unusual conditions?

Exercise	Max Score	Your Score	Comments
TOTAL:			

Was this the dog's first, second,
third, etc...class of the day?: _____

What did you learn from this _____
experience?: _____

(circle all that apply)

HOW DID YOU FEEL IN THE RING?   Rhythmical

    In Control   Forgot Footwork

    Nervous   Did more than my job

    Excited   Out of Rhythm

    Relaxed   Moved too slow

    Focused   Moved too fast

MATCH SHOW - LOG

Name of Match/Show: _____   Date: _____
Location (I/O): _____   Weather: _____
Ring Conditions: _____   Judge: _____
Class: _____   Your Goal: _____

Did you accomplish your goal?: _____
_____

Things dog did well: _____
_____

What things distracted your dog
that surprised you?: _____
_____

What proofs do you plan to do?: _____
_____

Not Perfect Yet: _____

Score (if any): [____]   ❦ Why did the dog lose points?
                          Score Breakdown   ❦ Did you notice your need for more proofing?
Leg or Title?: [____]   ❦ Did you correct at a Match
                                                       ❦ Were there unusual conditions?

Exercise	Max Score	Your Score	Comments
TOTAL:			

Was this the dog's first, second,
third, etc...class of the day?: _____

What did you learn from this _____
experience?: _____

(circle all that apply)

HOW DID YOU FEEL IN THE RING?   Rhythmical

                        In Control   Forgot Footwork

                        Nervous   Did more than my job

                        Excited   Out of Rhythm

                        Relaxed   Moved too slow

                        Focused   Moved too fast

MATCH SHOW - LOG

Name of Match/Show: _____ Date: _____
Location (I/O): _____ Weather: _____
Ring Conditions: _____ Judge: _____
Class: _____ Your Goal: _____
Did you accomplish your goal?: _____
_____

Things dog did well: _____
_____

What things distracted your dog
that surprised you?: _____
_____

What proofs do you plan to do?: _____
_____

Not Perfect Yet: _____

Score (if any): [____]

Score Breakdown

♣ Why did the dog lose points?
♣ Did you notice your need for more proofing?
♣ Did you correct at a Match
♣ Were there unusual conditions?

Leg or Title?: [____]

Exercise	Max Score	Your Score	Comments
TOTAL:			

Was this the dog's first, second,
third, etc...class of the day?: _____

What did you learn from this
experience?: _____

(circle all that apply)

HOW DID YOU FEEL IN THE RING?   Rhythmical

          In Control   Forgot Footwork

          Nervous   Did more than my job

          Excited   Out of Rhythm

          Relaxed   Moved too slow

          Focused   Moved too fast

MATCH SHOW − LOG

Name of Match/Show: _____ Date: _____
Location (I/O): _____ Weather: _____
Ring Conditions: _____ Judge: _____
Class: _____ Your Goal: _____
Did you accomplish your goal?: _____
_____

Things dog did well: _____
_____

What things distracted your dog
that surprised you?: _____
_____

What proofs do you plan to do?: _____
_____

Not Perfect Yet: _____

Score (if any): [   ]   Score Breakdown   ❧ Why did the dog lose points?
                                                            ❧ Did you notice your need for more proofing?
Leg or Title?: [   ]   ❧ Did you correct at a Match
                                                            ❧ Were there unusual conditions?

Exercise	Max Score	Your Score	Comments
TOTAL:			

Was this the dog's first, second,
third, etc...class of the day?: _____

What did you learn from this _____
experience?: _____

(circle all that apply)

HOW DID YOU FEEL IN THE RING?   Rhythmical

                          In Control   Forgot Footwork

                          Nervous   Did more than my job

                          Excited   Out of Rhythm

                          Relaxed   Moved too slow

                          Focused   Moved too fast

MATCH SHOW - LOG

Name of Match/Show: _____ Date: _____

Location (I/O): _____ Weather: _____

Ring Conditions: _____ Judge: _____

Class: _____ Your Goal: _____

Did you accomplish your goal?: _____

Things dog did well: _____

What things distracted your dog that surprised you?: _____

What proofs do you plan to do?: _____

Not Perfect Yet: _____

Score (if any): [____]

Leg or Title?: [____]

Score Breakdown

♣ Why did the dog lose points?
♣ Did you notice your need for more proofing?
♣ Did you correct at a Match
♣ Were there unusual conditions?

Exercise	Max Score	Your Score	Comments
TOTAL:			

Was this the dog's first, second, third, etc...class of the day?: _____

What did you learn from this experience?: _____

(circle all that apply)

HOW DID YOU FEEL IN THE RING?   Rhythmical

In Control   Forgot Footwork

Nervous   Did more than my job

Excited   Out of Rhythm

Relaxed   Moved too slow

Focused   Moved too fast

MATCH SHOW - LOG

Name of Match/Show: _____   Date: _____
Location (I/O): _____   Weather: _____
Ring Conditions: _____   Judge: _____
Class: _____   Your Goal: _____
Did you accomplish your goal?: _____
_____

Things dog did well: _____
_____

What things distracted your dog
that surprised you?: _____
_____

What proofs do you plan to do?: _____
_____

Not Perfect Yet: _____

Score (if any): [_____]   Score Breakdown

Leg or Title?: [_____]

- Why did the dog lose points?
- Did you notice your need for more proofing?
- Did you correct at a Match
- Were there unusual conditions?

Exercise	Max Score	Your Score	Comments
TOTAL:			

Was this the dog's first, second,
third, etc...class of the day?: _____

What did you learn from this _____
experience?: _____

(circle all that apply)

HOW DID YOU FEEL IN THE RING?   Rhythmical

                            In Control   Forgot Footwork

                            Nervous   Did more than my job

                            Excited   Out of Rhythm

                            Relaxed   Moved too slow

                            Focused   Moved too fast

MATCH SHOW - LOG

Name of Match/Show: _____ Date: _____
Location (I/O): _____ Weather: _____
Ring Conditions: _____ Judge: _____
Class: _____ Your Goal: _____
Did you accomplish your goal?: _____

Things dog did well: _____

What things distracted your dog that surprised you?: _____

What proofs do you plan to do?: _____

Not Perfect Yet: _____

Score (if any): [____]

Score Breakdown

- Why did the dog lose points?
- Did you notice your need for more proofing?
- Did you correct at a Match
- Were there unusual conditions?

Leg or Title?: [____]

Exercise	Max Score	Your Score	Comments
TOTAL:			

Was this the dog's first, second, third, etc...class of the day?: _____

What did you learn from this experience?: _____

(circle all that apply)

HOW DID YOU FEEL IN THE RING?   Rhythmical

        In Control   Forgot Footwork

        Nervous   Did more than my job

        Excited   Out of Rhythm

        Relaxed   Moved too slow

        Focused   Moved too fast